FOR
RELAXATION
IMAGERY
& INNER HEALING

30

SCRIPTS

FOR

RELAXATION
IMAGERY
& INNER HEALING

Edited by

Julie T. Lusk

 Whole Person Associates

Whole Person Associates
210 W Michigan St
Duluth, MN 55802-1908 218-727-0500

30 Scripts for Relaxation, Imagery & Inner Healing

Printed in the United States of America by Versa Press

10 9 8 7 6 5

Editor: Patrick Gross
Art Director: Joy Morgan Dey

Library of Congress Cataloging in Publication Data

92-80231

ISBN 0-938586-69-6

To Angie Tapin,
my constant source of inspiration,
my mother, my friend,

and to my husband Dave,
who gives me love and support
in all that I do.

Contents

Foreword

Relaxation and visualization heal the body, mind, and spirit. Progressive muscular relaxation and controlled breathing help relieve tension and stress. Guided imagery encourages people to experience internal harmony, to heal emotional and physical upsets, to increase body awareness, enhance relaxation, to get in touch with the healing source of energy for emotional and spiritual strength, to receive direction from their own inner guide, and to connect with the environment.

Many counselors, psychologists, teachers, ministers, and other professionals practice and use relaxation and guided imagery techniques in their training. However, most use only a few, limited varieties—their favorites. That's OK. These favorites get honed and perfected and help the trainer help others.

The problem in using only what we are familiar with is that we use only a small range of the options available to us and our clients. For this reason I asked leaders in the field to share their favorite relaxation and imagery exercises—their best and most effective.

I've compiled thirty scripts to expand your repertoire. I hope that these relaxation scripts, creative visualizations, and guided meditations will not only spark your imagination but stimulate your creativity as well. Please feel free to add your own thoughts. Mix and match ideas and approaches—IMPROVISE! Modify the scripts to suit the needs of your classes and your individual clients.

Julie T. Lusk
July 1992

Introduction

Many group leaders are aware of the benefits of guided imagery but have had little experience in the field. Here are some tips to help you use these scripts effectively.

Working with guided meditations

Everyone is different, so each person will experience guided imagery uniquely. These individual differences should be encouraged. During a guided meditation, some people will imagine vivid scenes, colors, images, or sounds while others will focus on what they are feeling. This is why a combination of sights, sounds, and feelings have been incorporated into the meditations. With practice, it is possible to expand your participants' range of awareness.

By careful selection of images you can help deepen their experience and cultivate their awareness in new areas that can enrich their lives. For instance, a person who is most comfortable in the visual area can be encouraged to stretch his or her awareness and increase his or her sensitivity to feelings and sounds. You'll find an example of how this can be done in the Flower Meditation script (Section 5).

Working with guided imagery is powerful and it is up to you to use this book responsibly and ethically. Leaders with little or no training in guided imagery can use these scripts with emotionally healthy people. Be careful, however, when presenting themes and techniques that are unfamiliar to you. Since people respond in a variety of ways to visualization, avoid generalizing about the benefits of any given script.

If your groups are composed of people who are emotionally ill or especially fragile, you should seek out special training or professional guidance before introducing them to visualizations.

Preparing the group or individual

Physical relaxation reduces anxiety, activates the creative right brain, and enhances the ability to concentrate on mental images. Some type of physical relaxation sequence should be used prior to any guided meditation. You'll find a variety of relaxation exercises to choose from in Section 1.

Breathing properly is essential for complete and total relaxation. Unfortunately, very few people take full breaths, especially when under stress. When a person consciously takes deep breaths, stress is reduced and the mind can remain calm and in control. It is important that people focus on their breathing, taking in full deep breaths through the nose.

Before beginning any guided meditation, briefly describe the images you will use and ask if they make anyone feel uncomfortable. People who are afraid of water may find images of ocean waves to be frightening rather than calming. Be prepared with an alternate image. Let participants know that if they become uncomfortable, they may, at any time, open their eyes and tune out the visualization.

As you read a script, people will follow you for a while and then drift off into their own imaginations. They will usually tune you back in later on. If they know this in advance, they won't feel as if they are failing by being inattentive. So tell them this is normal and to let it happen.

Choosing the right atmosphere

Select a room that has comfortable chairs for sitting or a carpeted floor for lying down. Close the door and shut the windows to block out distracting noise.

If possible, dim the lights to create a relaxing environment. Low lights enhance the ability to relax by blocking out visual distractions. If the room lights cannot be controlled to your satisfaction, bring along a lamp or a night light.

Adjust the thermostat so that the room temperature is warm and comfortable. If the room is too cool, it will be hard to relax and remain focused. Suggest that people wear a sweater or jacket if they think they may get cold.

If distractions occur—a noisy air conditioner, traffic, loud conversations—try raising your voice, using shorter phrases and fewer pauses, or incorporating the sounds into the guided meditation. For example, you might say, "Notice how the humming sounds of the air conditioner relax you more and more." Or, "If your mind begins to drift, gently bring it back to the sound of my voice."

Using your voice

Speak in a calm, comforting, and steady manner. Let your voice flow. Your voice should be smooth and somewhat monotonous. But don't whisper.

Start with your voice at a volume that can be easily heard. As the guided meditation progresses and as the participants' awareness increases, you may begin speaking more softly. As a person relaxes, hearing acuity increases. Bring your voice up when suggesting tension and bring it down when suggesting relaxation. Near the end of the guided meditation, return to using an easily heard volume. This will help participants come back.

You may tell participants to use a hand signal if they cannot hear you. Advise people with hearing impairments to sit close to you.

Pacing yourself

Read the guided meditations slowly, but not so slowly that you lose people. Begin at a conversational pace and slow down as the relaxation progresses. It's easy to go too fast, so take your time. Don't rush.

The ellipses . . . used throughout the book indicate a brief pause. Spaces between paragraphs suggest a longer pause.

Leader's notes and script divisions are printed in italics and should not be read out loud.

Give participants time to follow your instructions. If you suggest that they wiggle their toes, watch them do so, then wait for them to stop wiggling their toes before going on. When your participants are relaxed and engaged in the imagery process, they have tapped into their subconscious (slow, rich, imagery) mind—and they shouldn't be hurried.

When you're leading the meditation, you're still in your conscious (alert and efficient) mind. Pay careful attention to all participants. You may have to repeat an instruction if you see that people are not following you.

To help you with your volume and tone, pace and timing listen to a tape of yourself leading guided meditations.

As you reach the end of a meditation, help participants make the transition back to the present. Tell them to visualize their surroundings, to stretch, and to breathe deeply. Repeat these instructions until everyone is alert.

Using music

Using music to enhance relaxation is not a new idea. History is full of examples of medicine men and women, philosophers, priests, scientists, and musicians who used music to heal. In fact, music seems to be an avenue of communication for some people where no other avenues appear to exist.

Your music should be cued up and ready to go at the right volume before you start your meditation. Nothing ruins the atmosphere more quickly than having the leader fool around trying to get the audio tape going.

Jim Borling, a Board Certified Music Therapist, makes the following suggestions on selecting music.

Tips on Music Selection

• Custom select music for individual clients or classes whenever possible. Not everyone responds in a similar fashion to the same music.

• Matching a person's present emotional state with music is known as the ISO principle. If you can match the initial state and then gradually begin changing the music, the person's emotional state will change along with the music. If a person is agitated or angry, begin with fast-paced music, then change to slower-paced selections as relaxation deepens.

• Choose music that has flowing melodies rather than disjointed and fragmented melodies.

• Don't assume that the type of music you find relaxing will be relaxing to others. Have a variety of musical styles available and ask your clients for suggestions.

• Try using sounds from nature like ocean waves. Experiment with New Age music and Space music, much of which is appropriate for relaxation work. Classical music may be effective, especially movements that are marked Largo or Adagio.

• Adjust the volume so that it doesn't drown out your voice. On the other hand, music that is too soft may cause your listeners to strain to hear it.

• Select music based upon the mood desired. Sedative music is soothing and produces a contemplative mood. Stimulative music increases bodily energy and stimulates the emotions.

• Select music with a slow tempo and low pitch. The higher the pitch or frequency of sound, the more likely it will be irritating.

Processing the experience

You may wish to add to the richness of the guided meditations by asking participants afterwards to share their experiences with others. This can be facilitated by creating an atmosphere of trust. Ask the group open-ended questions that relate to the theme of the exercise. Be accepting and empathetic towards everyone. Respect everyone's comments and never be judgmental or critical, even if people express negative reactions.

Caution

Do not force people to participate in anything that may be uncomfortable for them. Give ample permission to everyone to only do things that feel safe. Tell them that if an image seems threatening, they can change it to something that feels right or they can stop the imaging process, stretch, and open their eyes. Emphasize to participants that they are in total control and are able to leave their image-filled subconscious mind and return to their alert rational conscious mind at any time they choose.

Advise participants that it is not safe to practice meditation or visualization while driving or operating machinery.

The relaxation scripts, guided meditations, and creative visualizations contained in this book are not intended to provide or be a substitute for medical or psychological advice on personal health matters. If this assistance is needed, consult a physician, therapist, or other health care professional. Neither the author nor Whole Person Press assumes responsibility for the improper use of the relaxation scripts, guided meditations, and creative visualizations contained in this book.

Taping the scripts

You may audiotape the scripts for your own personal or professional use. You may not, however, copy or distribute the scripts to others on audiotape or in written form.

Becoming Relaxed

Feeling calm, relaxed, and centered is a foundation for any guided meditation. In fact, relaxation is healing in and of itself. Physically relaxing the body first, before using guided imagery, increases people's ability to concentrate and allows their minds, hearts, and spirits to be more open to the meditation. A feeling of harmony often results.

For many people relaxation is a new experience. It is important that people practice the physical form of relaxation and spend ample time with it until feeling relaxed becomes natural and easy.

The exercises in this section focus on physical relaxation. Use them on their own or combine them with an imagery exercise from one of the other sections.

Progressively Relaxing while Sitting in a Chair

Julie T. Lusk

Time: 20 minutes

Designed for people sitting in chairs, this progressive relaxation exercise focuses on tensing and relaxing the different muscle groups.

If time is short, it is okay to tense and relax each side of the body separately without tensing both sides together, or just tense the right and left sides at the same time. You may eliminate counting to five after you become aware of the length of time needed for your clients to feel the tension and the relaxation and when they are comfortable with doing the exercise.

Note: Make sure participants have enough room to stretch their arms and legs straight out in front of them. Do not read the italicized headings out loud.

Script

Shoulders
> Close your eyes and begin feeling the sensation of relaxation.
>
> Take in a big breath and bring your shoulders up towards your ears.

Now drop your shoulders and release your breath.

Repeat, bring fresh air into your lungs, squeeze your shoulders up towards your ears, and hold . . . Now let your shoulders drop and relax as you release your breath.

Hands

Hold your right arm straight out in front of you and make a tight fist. Hold it, tighter and tighter. 1 . . . 2 . . . 3 . . . 4 . . . 5 . . . Relax. Drop your hand to your lap.

Once again hold your right arm straight out in front of you, make a tight fist, and hold. 1 . . . 2 . . . 3 . . . 4 . . . 5 . . . Relax and drop your hand to your lap.

This time, hold out your left arm and make a tight fist. 1 . . . 2 . . . 3 . . . 4 . . . 5 . . . Now relax. Let your arm relax completely, resting on your lap.

This time, hold both arms out, make two fists, and hold. 1 . . . 2 . . . 3 . . . 4 . . . 5 . . . Relax.

Lower Arms

Hold your right arm straight out and bend your hand backwards until your fingers point towards the ceiling. 1 . . . 2 . . . 3 . . . 4 . . . 5 . . . Relax. Let your arm fall to your lap.

Now hold your left arm straight out with your fingers pointing toward the ceiling. 1 ... 2 ... 3 ... 4 ... 5 ... Relax.

Notice the warm feeling in your arms.

This time, hold both arms out in the same manner as before. Feel the tension in the upper portion of your forearms. 1 ... 2 ... 3 ... 4 ... 5 ... Relax. Notice the feeling of relaxation in your arms ... warm and tingly.

Upper Arms

Now it is time to tense and relax your bicep muscles. Bring the fingers of your right hand to your right shoulder and tense your bicep muscle. 1 ... 2 ... 3 ... 4 ... 5 ... Relax. Let your arm fall to your lap.

Now bring the fingers of your left hand to your left shoulder and hold. 1 ... 2 ... 3 ... 4 ... 5 ... Relax.

This time, bring both hands to your shoulders and tense the biceps. Tense 1 ... 2 ... 3 ... 4 ... 5 ... Relax.

Notice the feeling of relaxation in your arms ... warm, heavy, and comfortable.

Thighs

Draw your attention to your thighs.

Press your knees together so that the parts of
your legs above the knees are touching. 1 . . .
2 . . . 3 . . . 4 . . . 5 . . . Relax.

Lower Legs

Focus your attention on your legs . . . Hold your
right leg straight out, point your toes forward,
then tense your leg. 1 . . . 2 . . . 3 . . . 4 . . . 5 . . .
Relax. Let your foot gently fall to the floor.

Now hold your left leg straight out, point your
toes, and tense. 1 . . . 2 . . . 3 . . . 4 . . . 5 . . . Relax.

This time, hold both legs straight out with your
toes pointing forward. Notice the tension in your
calf muscles. 1 . . . 2 . . . 3 . . . 4 . . . 5 . . . Relax.

Below the Kneecap

Shift your attention to below your kneecap.
Hold your right leg straight out and point your
toes toward your head. 1 . . . 2 . . . 3 . . . 4 . . .
5 . . . Relax.

This time, hold your left leg straight out and
point your toes toward your head. 1 . . . 2 . . .
3 . . . 4 . . . 5 . . . Relax.

Hold both legs out and point your toes. Focus
on the area below your kneecap. 1 . . . 2 . . . 3 . . .
4 . . . 5 . . . Relax. You are feeling more and more
relaxed.

Notice that your legs and arms feel heavy,

warm, and relaxed. Resolve to keep them still and relaxed.

Abdomen

Now concentrate on relaxing your abdominal region. Draw in your abdominal muscles as tightly as you can. 1 . . . 2 . . . 3 . . . 4 . . . 5 . . . Relax, feeling all of the knots inside letting go.

Now push your abdominal muscles outward as far as you can. 1 . . . 2 . . . 3 . . . 4 . . . 5 . . . Relax. You are feeling more and more relaxed.

Chest

Shift your attention to your chest. Take in a deep breath and hold. 1 . . . 2 . . . 3 . . . 4 . . . 5 . . . Let all of the air rush out, and relax.

Neck

Now concentrate on relaxing your neck. It is important to learn to relax this area because a lot of tension accumulates here.

Tip your head directly to the right side, moving your right ear toward your right shoulder. Be careful not to strain. 1 . . . 2 . . . 3 . . . 4 . . . 5.

Bring your head back up to center. Let it wobble until it comes to a comfortable resting position.

Now let your left ear drop towards your left shoulder. 1 . . . 2 . . . 3 . . . 4 . . . 5.

Center your head and let it wobble until
comfortable.

To relax the muscles in the front of your neck,
bend your head forward and bring your chin
towards your chest. 1 . . . 2 . . . 3 . . . 4 . . . 5 . . .
Relax. Let your head wobble.

Mouth

To relax your mouth, press your lips tightly
together. 1 . . . 2 . . . 3 . . . 4 . . . 5 . . . Relax, letting
your lips part slightly.

Now bring your tongue upward and press it
against the roof of your mouth. 1 . . . 2 . . . 3 . . .
4 . . . 5 . . . Relax, letting your lips part slightly.

Jaw

To loosen up your jaw, open your mouth and
move your jaw up and down and back and
forth, working out all tension . . . Relax. Let your
lips part slightly.

Nose and Cheeks

To relax your nose and cheeks, wrinkle up your
nose and hold. 1 . . . 2 . . . 3 . . . 4 . . . 5 . . . Relax.

Eyes

To relax your eyes, squeeze them tightly
together. 1 . . . 2 . . . 3 . . . 4 . . . 5 . . . Relax.

Forehead

To relax your forehead, frown and push your
eyebrows downward. 1 . . . 2 . . . 3 . . . 4 . . . 5 . . .
Relax.

Now draw your eyebrows upward. 1 . . . 2 . . .
3 . . . 4 . . . 5 . . . Relax.

All Over

It is now time to mentally scan your entire body.
If you notice any remaining tension, give that
area permission to relax and let go.

You are now very, very relaxed . . . Enjoy this
feeling . . . Allow this feeling to sink in all over.

Pause

*You may continue on with a visualization exercise from
another section of this book, or say the following:*

Start to picture the room you are in . . . the walls,
the ceiling, the floor.

Describe different aspects of the room.

When you can picture the room completely,
open your eyes and stretch.

Repeat the above instructions until everyone is alert.

Breathing for Relaxation and Health

Julie T. Lusk

Time: 10 minutes

Effective relaxation requires proper breathing. In this script, participants concentrate on their breathing by focusing on what their bodies are doing as they take in deep breaths, hold them, and slowly exhale.

Note: The following information will help your participants understand the importance of slow, deep, rhythmic breathing. You may wish to present it as a mini-lecture prior to using this script.

> Breathe in through the nose, not the mouth. The nose filters out pollutants and it moistens and warms the air.
>
> Breathing should be natural, smooth, easy, slow, and silent. Exhaling fully and deeply is the first step to perfect breathing. It stimulates the functioning of the brain cells and rids the system of stale air and carbon dioxide. Exhaling creates ample room for the incoming air.
>
> Inhaling is equally important. The heart relaxes when you inhale, and life-giving energy is taken into the entire system.
>
> Oxygenation of the body through proper breathing is essential to physical health and well-being. Oxygen is necessary for development of all organs in the body. Red blood cells are completely renewed every 120 days. The most essential element for accomplishing this reconstruction is not food, but oxygen.

11

Shallow and irregular breathing results in an insufficient oxygen supply, the accumulation of bodily wastes and poisons, and inadequate functioning of all body organs and tissues. Breathing that is slow, smooth, and deep leads to a clear and alert mind.

Script

Close your eyes ... Focus your mind on your breath ... Just follow the air as it goes in ... and as it goes out.

Feel it as it comes in ... and as it goes out ... If your mind begins to wander, just bring it back to your breath.

Feel your stomach rise ... your ribs expand ... and your collar-bone rise ... Breathe in naturally and slowly.

On your next exhalation, release all the air from your lungs without straining ... Let it all go ... Let it all out ... Prepare your lungs to receive fresh oxygen.

Now take in a full, deep breath and let the air go to the bottom of your lungs ... Feel your stomach rise ... your chest expand, and the collar-bone area fill.

Now empty your lungs from top to bottom . . .
Let all the air out . . . Compress your stomach to
squeeze out all the stale air and carbon dioxide.
Squeeze out every bit of air . . . Let it all go.

Take in another deep breath . . . As you breathe
in, your diaphragm expands and massages all
the internal organs in the abdominal area . . .
aiding your digestion.

Breathe out . . . Relax . . . Feel the knots in your
stomach untie . . . Let go.

Breathe in . . . Your diaphragm is stimulating
your vagus nerve, slowing down the beating of
your heart . . . relaxing you.

Breathe out . . . Let it all go . . . relax . . . relax
more and more . . . Breathing heals you . . .
calms you . . . soothes you.

Breathe in again, fully and completely. Oxygen
is entering your blood stream, nourishing all
your organs and cells . . . protecting you.

Breathe out . . . Release all the poisons and
toxins with your breath. Your breath is cleansing
you . . . healing you.

Breathe in.

Now imagine exhaling confusion . . .
and inhaling clarity.

Imagine exhaling darkness . . .
and inhaling light.

Imagine exhaling hatred . . .
and inhaling love.

Exhaling anxiety . . .
and inhaling peace.

Exhaling selfishness . . .
and inhaling generosity.

Exhaling guilt . . .
and inhaling forgiveness.

Exhaling weakness . . .
and inhaling courage.

Breathe in through your nose and sigh out
through your mouth. Let the air stay out of your
lungs as long as it is comfortable, and then take
another breath.

Let your breath return to its normal and natural
pace. Continue to breathe in slowly, smoothly,
and deeply . . . Your breathing is steady, easy,
silent.

Each time you exhale . . . allow yourself to feel

peaceful . . . calm . . . and completely relaxed . . .
If your mind wanders, bring your attention back
to your breath.

Pause

*You may continue on with a visualization exercise from
another section of this book, or say the following:*

Stretch and open your eyes, feeling refreshed,
rejuvenated, alert, and fully alive.

Repeat the above instructions until everyone is alert.

1 to 10

Julie T. Lusk

Time: 5 minutes

In this brief script, participants lie on their backs and tense their muscles as they count from 1 to 10, then release the tension as they count back down to 1.

Script

Begin by closing your eyes . . . and releasing the air in your lungs.

Take in a full, deep breath through your nose, allowing your lungs to fill up completely, letting the air go all the way in . . . and then sighing it out through your open mouth. Release all of the tiredness, tension, and negativity with your breath.

Take in another deep breath . . . And sigh it out. Take your time . . . Breathing in . . . and out.

Pause for 20 seconds

Now let your breath return to normal.

In a minute or so, I will begin to count from 1 to 10. As I count up, you will slowly begin tensing all the muscles throughout your body: your arms and legs, your torso and back, your shoulders and face. At the count of 5, your body will be half way to being tense all over.

By the count of 10, you will feel tension and tightness throughout your entire body.

Then I will count backwards from 10 to 1. As I count down, you will slowly release the tension in your body. By the count of 5, you will be half way to being completely relaxed. At the count of 1, your body will be completely relaxed. Then you will take in a big breath and then sigh it out.

Now sense how your body feels as it presses firmly against the floor. Become aware of how your body is feeling right now—your legs, back, arms, and head. You are becoming acutely aware of how you are feeling in your physical body right now. Physically . . . how your body feels to you. Just become aware.

Let's begin. 1 . . . add a little tension . . . 2 . . . add some more . . . 3 . . . 4 . . . 5 . . . you are half way there . . . 6 . . . 7 . . . 8 . . . 9 . . . and 10.

You are all the way there now. Feel the tension. Know it and experience it completely so that you will be able to recognize muscular tension and tightness later on.

9 . . . relax a little bit . . . 8 . . . a little bit more . . .
7 . . . 6 . . . 5 . . . you are half way there . . . 4 . . .
3 . . . 2 . . . and 1.

Dissolve and release all of the muscular tension
and tiredness. Let go completely . . . Experience
the feeling of being completely relaxed and
calm . . . Soak it in . . . Learn to recognize the
feeling of relaxation.

If you still feel some muscular tension, you will
find that you can relax even more if your mind
gives your body permission to relax. Let those
spots relax now by mentally giving yourself
permission to relax . . . It's OK to relax . . . Just
let go.

Take in a long, deep breath and sigh it out,
letting the air rush out through your open
mouth. Keep the air out of your body until you
are no longer comfortable, then take in another
deep breath and sigh it out completely . . .
Notice that you can relax more and more, each
time you exhale.

Pause for 20 seconds

Now let your breath return to normal.

Notice that you feel as if you are sinking into the
floor. Let the floor support and hold you, safely
and securely.

Your body feels as if it is being supported
entirely by the floor. Every time you breathe out,
feel more and more relaxed, calm, and serene.

Now draw your attention to your mind . . .
Notice what thoughts are drifting through your
mind right now . . . Let your mind and thoughts
become silent and still so that you can begin to
center in and concentrate more.

If your mind begins to wander, gently bring
your attention back to the sound of my voice or
to the motion of your breathing.

Now notice how your emotional self is feeling
right now. What kind of mood are you in? Try
not to judge your mood, just recognize and
accept what you are naturally experiencing at
this moment.

Each time you exhale, notice that you feel more
and more settled and are feeling a sense of
harmony and balance occurring within your
body, mind, mood, and spirit. Feel this sense of
balance within your body . . . mind . . . and
emotions.

Pause

*You may continue on with a visualization exercise from
another section of this book, or say the following:*

Start to picture the room you are in . . . the walls, the ceiling, the floor.

Describe different aspects of the room.

When you can picture the room completely, open your eyes and stretch.

Repeat the above instructions until everyone is alert.

The Magic Ball

John Heil

Time: 20 minutes

In this visualization script, participants imagine they each possess a magic ball that travels over, under, and through their bodies, relaxing their muscles as it goes.

This script draws on the concepts of centering and energy flow that are found in yoga, Zen, and Tai Chi. It is a useful technique for bridging passive and active meditative methods.

The *Magic Ball* may be developed further by giving it special properties of warmth, movement, shape, and penetration. This is a great exercise to use for soothing sore muscles or rejuvenating tired ones.

Script

Please close your eyes . . . Wiggle around a little until you find a way of sitting that is completely comfortable.

Relax your entire body to the best of your ability . . . Feel that comfortable heaviness that accompanies relaxation.

Breathe easily and freely . . . in and out . . . Notice how the relaxation increases as you exhale . . . Feel the relaxation.

Now breathe in and fill your lungs . . . inhale deeply and hold your breath . . . Study the tension . . . Now exhale, let the walls of your chest grow loose and push the air out automatically.

Continue relaxing and breathe freely and gently . . . Feel the relaxation and enjoy it.

With the rest of your body as relaxed as possible, fill your lungs again. Breathe in deeply and hold it again . . . That's fine.

Breathe out and appreciate the relief.

Now breathe normally. Continue relaxing your chest and let the relaxation spread to your back, shoulders, neck, and arms . . . Let go . . . and enjoy the relaxation.

Now pay attention to your abdominal muscles, your stomach area. Tighten your stomach muscles outward and make your abdomen hard. Notice the tension . . . and relax. Let the muscles loosen and notice the contrast.

Once more, press and tighten your stomach muscles. Hold the tension . . . and relax. Notice the general well-being that comes with relaxing your stomach.

Now draw your stomach in, pull the muscles

right in and feel the tension this way . . . Now
relax again . . . Let your stomach out.

Continue breathing normally and easily and feel
the gentle massaging action all over your chest
and stomach.

Pause for 15 seconds

Now pull your stomach in again and hold the
tension . . . Now push out and tense like that,
hold the tension.

Once more pull in and feel the tension . . . Now
relax your stomach fully. Let the tension
dissolve as the relaxation grows deeper.

Each time you breathe out, notice how your
chest and your stomach relax more and more . . .
Try and let go of all contractions anywhere in
your body.

You will find that you may move to a deeper
state of relaxation by simply concentrating on
relaxing . . . Relax your feet . . . ankles . . . calves
. . . shins . . . knees . . . thighs . . . buttocks . . .
and hips.

Feel the heaviness of your lower body as you
relax still further . . . Now spread the relaxation
to your stomach . . . waist . . . lower back . . . Let
go more and more. Feel that relaxation all
over . . . Let it proceed to your upper back . . .

chest . . . shoulders and arms and right to the tips of your fingers. Keep relaxing more and more deeply.

Pause for 15 seconds

Allow your mind's eye to open now . . . Looking deeply within yourself . . . locate your center. This will appear as a ball of awareness situated in your abdomen . . . at the bottom of the space that fills with each breath.

Now imagine a ball resting at your center . . . Slowly and deliberately the ball moves from your center to the point of your right hip . . . soothing and massaging your muscles as it goes.

Continuing along, the ball moves down the outside of your thigh until it reaches the knee. Here the ball moves across the back of the leg and around the front just below the kneecap.

Continuing on down the outer edge of the calf, it passes the ankle and moves along the outside of the foot . . . finally coming to rest for an instant on the tip of the small toe. Then moving in succession to the fourth and the third and the second toes, it again rests for an instant on the big toe.

It then proceeds along the arch . . . moves past the ankle, goes up the inner edge of the calf past the knee and along the inside of the thigh . . .

and then comes to rest back at the center . . . that point of awareness at the bottom of the space that fills with each breath.

From here the ball proceeds down along the inside of the left thigh, moves past the knee, continues along the inside of the calf, past the ankle and past the arch of your foot . . . then comes to rest for an instant on the big toe . . . Then it moves onto the second . . . third . . . and fourth toes . . . and comes to rest on the small toe.

It then moves along the outer edge of the foot . . . past the ankle . . . along the calf to the knee. And there the ball moves under the back of the knee and over the front just below the kneecap . . . And then it proceeds along the outside of the thigh and comes to rest at the center . . . at the bottom of the space that fills with each breath.

And now descending through the abdomen gently and smoothly . . . continuing to soothe and massage the muscles as it goes . . . the ball comes to rest at the base of the spine.

Pausing for an instant, it starts to slowly move up the spinal cord . . . It pauses at the heart and then finally comes to rest at the throat.

From here it proceeds to the left along the outside of the neck . . . past the point of the shoulder and along the back of the arm . . . the forearm . . . and into the hand . . . entering the little finger first . . . and then each of the fingers in succession . . . until it finally comes to rest for an instant at the tip of the thumb.

And moving once again . . . the ball continues past the hand . . . along the inside of the forearm . . . past the elbow . . . and along the upper arm.

And now moving slowly across the chest . . . the ball comforts the muscles as it goes by . . . Reaching the opposite arm . . . it travels down the inside of the arm past the elbow . . . along the forearm . . . and into the hand . . . coming to rest for an instant at the tip of the thumb . . . before proceeding to each of the fingers in succession . . . until finally moving out of the little finger and along the back of the forearm and arm . . . up along the edge of the neck to the throat.

Moving now . . . up to the center of the head . . . at the base of the brain . . . the ball comes to rest behind the eyes . . . between the ears. And now this one ball splits into many balls . . . with each moving to a different area of the face and head . . . continuing for a while . . . an exhilarating surge of activity . . . before all unite once again and come to rest at the base of the brain.

Pause

You may continue on with a visualization exercise from another section of this book, or say the following:

And now . . . count backwards silently to yourself from five to one . . . When you reach the count of one . . . open your eyes. When you arise you will feel relaxed, refreshed, and invigorated.

Repeat the above instructions until everyone is alert.

Total Relaxation

Karen Sothers

Time: 10 minutes

An eclectic introduction to some of the most popular relaxation techniques, *Total Relaxation* includes breathing, progressive relaxation, visualization, and body scanning. Use a part or all of this script as a short relaxation exercise prior to a guided meditation in one of the other sections of the book.

Script

Part 1

Begin by taking in a deep breath . . . Now, as you exhale, let your eyes close . . . Feel that this time is just for you.

Take three deep abdominal breaths. Feel as if you are releasing all the thoughts and tension of the day with each exhalation . . . Allow your abdomen to expand on the inhalation . . . and contract on the exhalation. Let go of tension and tightness as you exhale

Expand . . . and contract. Expand . . . and contract. Expand . . . and contract.

Part 2

To enter into a deeper state of relaxation, you will soon tense the entire muscular system until your whole body is tense. Then you will exhale and relax all at once.

Shift your attention to your feet . . . Curl your toes and feel tension spread into your calves. Press your knees together and feel the tightness in your thighs. Squeeze your buttocks and tighten your pelvic area. Make two fists and feel the tension spread into your arms. Raise your shoulders and create tension in your neck. Take a deep breath and tighten your stomach and chest. Tense your jaw and gently squeeze your eyes shut. Experience tension all over your body.

Now exhale and let your body relax all at once . . . Let go and unwind . . . Feel the warmth and heaviness of deep relaxation penetrate your muscles. Feel your muscles releasing . . . letting go . . . unwinding.

Relax your face . . . Feel your forehead smooth out . . . Soften your eyes . . . Relax the spot between your eyebrows . . . Let all facial expression fall away.

Relax the corners of your mouth . . . Allow your jaw to hang slack with enough space for a pencil to fit through . . . Allow your neck to be so relaxed that a gentle breeze blowing through the room would rock your head from side to side.

Lower your shoulders . . . Relax your hands, turning your palms up . . . Relax your forearms and upper arms.

Allow your chest to sink down deep into the floor or chair . . . Let your stomach be so soft that it gently expands on the inhalation and contracts on the exhalation, receiving each breath freely. Allow your hips and buttock muscles to let go and unwind.

As you sink down deeper into relaxation, let go of your thighs and calves . . . Let your knees separate . . . Relax your feet and toes.

Part 3

Return to taking long, deep breaths.

Picture your lungs and heart . . . Feel their pace becoming slow and free of tension . . . See if in this stillness you can feel your heart beating.

If you would like, you can place your hand on your pulse to feel the rhythm, or just imagine what your heart would look like as it beats.

Begin to slow your breathing tempo to approximately three heart beats to each

inhalation and five heartbeats to each
exhalation.

Continue taking deep breaths. Feel and picture
your heart beating . . . three heart beats as you
inhale and five beats as you exhale.

With each breath, feel yourself breathing-in
relaxation . . . With each breath, feel yourself
release tension and tiredness . . . inhaling
relaxation . . . exhaling tension.

Bring your attention to the organs of your
abdominal cavity. Without trying to guess their
exact location, picture your stomach and
intestines . . . See your kidneys, liver, bladder,
and reproductive organs . . . As you relax each
organ, picture or sense the deep tensions
dissolving at your mental suggestion to relax.

Now visualize your brain and imagine the
steady rhythm of your breath cleaning it of all
tension . . . dissolving thoughts with
exhalation . . . For now, feel that you have
completely let go.

Imagine that your mind is like a clear blue sky
with thoughts floating by like white fluffy
clouds . . . Feel your body and mind sinking
deeper and deeper into relaxation . . . deeper
and deeper . . . letting go and unwinding with
each exhalation.

Part 4

Now send your mind as far as it can go from your everyday life. Leave all of your anxiety, worries, obligations, and responsibilities . . . Create a strong mental picture of where you can be completely free and relaxed . . . completely at peace.

Perhaps you will imagine a sunny beach or grassy meadow . . . a majestic mountain . . . or a favorite room . . . Create in your mind's eye, your ideal spot for relaxation in as much detail as you can image.

Use all your senses. See the sights and colors . . . Hear the sounds . . . Feel the textures . . . Smell the air . . . Experience your ideal spot for relaxation.

Retreat into your personal sanctuary leaving only your body lying or sitting on the floor in a state devoid of all fears of the future and all regrets over the past.

Feel secure in the knowledge that you are at home within yourself . . . Allow this inner silence to restore your being on all levels.

For a moment let yourself drift . . . For a moment be aware of how deeply relaxed your mind and body feel right now . . . Remind yourself that

you can create these feelings on your own
during your daily activities.

Periodically during the day, scan your body
and then inhale relaxation and exhale tension
and tightness. Your breath is a powerful tool to
help you relax.

Pause

*You may continue on with a visualization exercise from
another section of this book, or say the following:*

Very gently and slowly prepare yourself for the
world of activity . . . Enjoy making this
transition from relaxation to activation.

Begin by deepening your inhalation . . . Be
aware of how your body, mind, and spirit feel
right now.

Allow this awareness to sink down into your
memory so you can recall these feelings during
your daily activities.

Gently stretch your body in a way that feels
most natural for you . . . Whenever you feel
ready, you can open your eyes feeling relaxed
and alert.

Repeat the above instructions until everyone is alert.

Nature and the Environment

Being connected to the natural world—the ocean, forest, sky, and mountains—is for most people both relaxing and healthy. The guided meditations in this section help people find their connection with the natural world and thereby learn about forgiveness and love.

Note: Before beginning any script, describe to the participants what images you will use. If they make anyone feel uncomfortable, select an alternate script.

The Sea

Don R. Powell

Time: 5 minutes

In this script, participants relax by taking an imaginary journey along a beach, listening to the birds and waves and watching a brilliant sunset.

Script

Make yourself as comfortable as possible. Close your eyes and become aware of which parts of your body are feeling tense and which parts are relaxed.

Now take a few deep breaths, taking the air in through your nose, holding it momentarily . . . and then slowly exhaling through your nose . . . And with each exhale, you will find yourself relaxing more and more deeply, more and more completely.

Take the air in and let the air out. Allowing yourself to relax . . . relax . . . relax.

In a few moments, I am going to describe a very vivid scene in which you will picture yourself walking along a beach. I want you to imagine this scene as though you are there experiencing not only the sights, but the sounds, smells, tastes, and touches.

It is a bright summer day. It is late in the day. You decide to go for a walk along the beach. The sun is radiating warmth and comfort as it shines boldly. The sky is crystal clear without a cloud in sight. The grains of sand beneath your feet shine from the sunlight and warm the soles of your feet. The sound of the waves beating against the shore echoes in the air.

You feel the warm, light breeze brush against your face as you walk onward. Far off in the distance, you can hear the cries of sea gulls . . . You watch them glide through the sky, swoop down into the sea, and then fly off once again.

As you walk further along the shore, you decide to rest. You sit down on a mound of pure white sand and gaze out at the sea, staring intently at the rhythmic, methodical motion of the waves rolling into shore .

Each wave breaks against the coast . . . rises slowly upward along the beach, leaving an aura of white foam, and then slowly retreats back out to sea, only to be replaced by another wave that crashes against the shore . . . works its way up the beach . . . then slowly retreats back out to sea.

With each motion of the wave as it glides in and as it glides out, you find yourself feeling more and more relaxed, more and more calm . . . more and more serene.

The waves are gliding in . . . and the waves are gliding out . . . You feel more and more calm . . . Continue to watch the waves glide in . . . and out.

Now, as you stare off into the distance, you see that the sun is beginning to sink into the horizon. The sun is sinking down and you feel more and more relaxed as you see its movement going down . . . down . . . down.

The sky is turning brilliant colors of red . . . orange . . . yellow . . . green . . . blue . . . and purple . . . As the sun sets, sinking down . . . down . . . down . . . into the horizon, you feel very relaxed and soothed. You watch the sun as it sinks down . . . down . . . down.

The beating of the waves, the smell and taste of the sea, the salt, the cries of the gulls, the warmth against your body—all these sights, sounds, and smells leave you feeling very soothed, very calm, very serene.

Relax . . . relax . . . relax.

Pause

In a few moments, I will count from one to three. When I reach the count of three, your eyes will open and you will feel completely refreshed and totally relaxed.

1 . . . 2 . . . 3.

Repeat the above instruction until everyone is alert.

Simply Sailing

Deborah and Bob Haywood

Time: 25 minutes

In this script, participants imagine setting sail from a quiet dock, experiencing the sea with all its beauty and challenges, and reaching an island paradise. They are invited to release unnecessary personal "baggage" and return to the dock with a newfound energy.

Script

Preparing to let go

You are about to have a wonderful sailing experience on a forty-foot sailboat. As you prepare to let go, let yourself relax.

Close your eyes . . . take three slow, deep breaths . . . Breathe in, hold your breath . . . breathe out . . . Breathe in, hold . . . breathe out . . . Breathe in, hold . . . breathe out.

See yourself at a quiet dock in a beautiful marina somewhere on the coast . . . Notice the weather. Is it sunny or cloudy . . . breezy or still?

As you get ready to cast off and sail outward to

a new place, notice how much you are looking forward to this journey.

As you stand on the dock waiting to depart, you become aware of a desire to simplify your life on this trip . . . You'd like to go free and with only the bare essentials. As you look at all the things you have brought with you, notice what they are and think about what you might be willing to leave behind on the dock.

See yourself sorting out your unnecessary luggage and leaving it safely on the dock.

As you stand there, try to get in touch with any emotional luggage that you want to leave behind with your unnecessary luggage . . . Any feelings, attitudes, or emotions that you don't want to take along with you on this special trip, leave them on the dock as well.

If you have any difficulties or conflicts in your life at this time, give yourself permission to leave these conflicts behind with your other luggage . . . See yourself leaving them.

Take in a smooth, deep breath . . . and, for now, let everything go. Leave all that luggage behind, and if you need it when you get back, it will all still be there.

Now see yourself on the boat, and see the things

you've left behind. You are now ready to go. A bit freer, a bit less burdened. Notice your relief and sense of release. Feel your peacefulness growing.

Breathe deeply ... Now relax ... Breathe deeply again ... Relax.

Becoming more aware

Now you are ready to sail and move into a time of increased awareness.

See yourself on your boat leaving the dock, beginning to move through the water, slowly ... smoothly. Before long you are on the sea, sailing.

After a while, you can hardly see the land you left. The sea is calm; the winds are brisk and steady. The boat moves well through the sea. See yourself either steering at the helm or relaxing on the deck.

As your body continues to relax, be aware of your muscles and how they feel. Let yourself relax even more. Let go. Let go of it all.

Remember, you have very little with you and that feels good. Be aware of the world around you. Feel the breeze on your body ... and the warmth of the sun.

What can you see? . . . What sounds do you hear? Notice the fullness of the sails and the sounds they make.

You are becoming more relaxed and comfortable. If you are alone, take a moment to enjoy your own company . . . How does that feel? . . . If you are not alone, notice who is with you . . . See them, sense them. Be with them if you choose.

Take a deep breath . . . hold it . . . and let it out.

What is your energy like? As you are sailing, be aware of your energy and sense your pleasure. Live for a few moments in this scene of peace, contentment, and well-being.

Alone

Now you are coming into an experience of pleasant solitude.

Your boat is now anchored a little way offshore of a small, secluded island, and you prepare to enjoy the island by yourself. Find yourself moving from the boat to the island in whatever way you wish.

You are alone and have received a special gift within you that feels comforting, alive, powerful, healing.

It is hot, but there are plenty of palm trees to shade you from the sun. Strung between two palm trees is an inviting hammock. Climb in and let yourself swing gently.

How does the hammock feel against your skin? . . . How does it feel to be alone? Does the solitude feel good? Are you lonely? If so, for whom?

Nothing else matters except this moment and this place. Breathe deeply, hold your breath . . . and let it out.

Notice what's *within* you in your solitude. Notice what's *around* you in your solitude.

When you are ready, take a walk on the beach . . . Notice the sea shells scattered around in the sand. There aren't a lot of shells to choose from, but if you look carefully enough you can find a special one.

Reach down and pick it up. Examine it; enjoy it. Feel the sun on your back. Walk a bit further then glance up and look down your beach about a hundred yards ahead.

As you look, you notice an item sticking out of the sand. You stroll up to it and discover that it's a chest of some sort.

You look at it and know instinctively that there is a special gift inside it for you. Dig the chest out of the sand and open it.

Find your gift and cherish it . . . Imagine its texture, shape, and design. What makes it so special for you . . . What qualities give it meaning?

When you are finished appreciating your gift, begin to make your way back up the beach. Wade in the warm water and feel it caress your legs . . . Wade in a bit further, and when you're ready, begin to swim to your boat.

Transcending

Now you are preparing to experience a new, different reality.

As you swim comfortably and leisurely, prepare yourself to transcend. Looking below, you see, not too far off, a beautiful underwater reef.

You can look at the reef from on top of the water, or, if you are comfortable, you can dive down towards the reef and see it from below. You will find that if you swim either on top of or under this special sea, you will have no trouble breathing and will be free to explore as you wish.

You feel no fear as you begin to explore. Look at

the colors of the reef . . . the blues, the greens.
Look at the sunlight shining through the water.

Drift with the gentle movement of the sea
bottom. Notice the different kinds of sea life . . .
brightly colored reef fish, a large brown grouper,
an eel . . . Look off to one side and see a
dolphin. Swim a little further and cross paths
with a lazy sea turtle.

Now look up above or around you and see a
pelican floating on the surface. Easily and gently
find yourself becoming one of these creatures, or
become a part of the ocean bottom.

Become that creature or part that you admire
and honor and spend a few moments enjoying
your new, natural environment. Reflect now on
the qualities that allow you to enjoy what you
have suddenly, magically become.

Tranquility disturbed

It's time to move on. Storm clouds are on the
horizon.

As your unique transcending and swimming
experience closes, find yourself back on your
boat . . . Rest for a moment . . . Notice the
blessings of where you are and where you've
been.

Now prepare to move on and sail away once

more. Raise your sail and move away from your private island.

Soon, you notice the winds picking up. Sense the wind in your face, feel the seas building, and the boat heeling, racing faster through the waves. You are excited, but not at all scared or frightened.

The skies begin to darken and lightning begins to flash as a squall approaches. Feel what this is like . . . staying with the storm for a few moments, fully aware of yourself and the elements.

Now almost as suddenly as the storm began, the storm passes and the sun comes forth and the winds calm down.

You have survived. What feelings are you having after the storm's passage . . . Reflect for a moment on storms you have experienced in your own life . . . What got you through those storms?

Think of people or qualities that have helped you survive . . . Perhaps a storm is waiting on your horizon. Notice your confidence and energy from this experience. How does that make you feel? . . . How do you feel about surviving that storm? . . . Stay with this reflection for a moment.

Now come back and relax into the scene of your strong boat sailing on a peaceful sea.

Returning

Your trip is nearing its conclusion. The sky is clear and the wind is brisk. The sun is bright and your sense of well-being is strong. As you look beyond the bow, low on the horizon, you see land. It is your destination.

How are you feeling as you near the end of your journey? Think about your destination. Where is it? . . . What does it look like? . . . Who or what is waiting for you when you arrive . . . What do you *want* waiting for you when you arrive?

Imagine all the things you left on the dock . . . Decide what you will pick up and take with you and what you will leave untouched and unneeded. Spend a few moments with these images and reflect on the unnecessary burdens, tangible and emotional, you no longer need to carry.

What is it you want to savor and allow to touch your spirit again? . . . Enjoy these feelings and identify what you need to do to feel finished with this sailing journey.

The land is growing nearer. Discover your prevailing mood.

Savor this moment, this sailing experience ...
Having let go ... having become more
aware ... having spent time alone and having
discovered your special core within ... having
transcended and been part of all ... having
survived the challenge of a brief storm ... and
having returned ... you stand refreshed,
renewed, centered, energized, and rested ...
and you bring all this energy and renewal back
with you on your return.

Pause

When you are ready, return your attention
back to this room, stretch and open your eyes.

Repeat the above instruction until everyone is alert.

A Day in the Life of Another Creature

Michael Arloski

Time: 20 minutes

In this relaxation and visualization script, participants let go of tension and then explore the wildlife found around a pond, first through the perspective of an animal or insect, and then from the human perspective.

This is a good exercise to discuss afterwards with the group. Explore both the experience of relaxation and the visualizations. Have people share what creatures they became. Have them point out similarities between the activities of the creatures and of themselves. You might even suggest that they act out the movements and sounds of their creatures.

Script

This is a time to let go . . . This is a time to reconnect with yourself and with the world of nature that you are a part of.

Allow yourself to relax while sitting in a comfortable chair that supports you, or by lying down on your back on a comfortable surface . . . Close your eyes and become aware of your body . . . Scan over your body from head to toe and visualize each part.

See each part of your body in your mind's eye.
Notice the feelings, or lack of feeling, that you
experience as you do this . . . Don't work at
it . . . Let it happen . . . Allow yourself to let
go . . . Give yourself permission . . . Allow
yourself to concentrate, but in a very passive
way.

Without changing it, become aware of your
breath . . . Follow a breath in through your
nose, down into your lungs . . . and back out
again. Follow the life-giving air of the world that
sustains us all.

Now take a deeper breath, drawing the air in
through your nose and filling your lungs
completely . . . hold your breath . . . and now
exhale.

Imagine the tension flowing out with your
breath. Follow the motion of your own
breathing. Let it set a rhythm for you. Pace
yourself to it.

Perhaps you will want to breathe in saying
silently to yourself . . . "I am," and then
exhaling saying . . . "relaxed" . . . "I am . . .
relaxed." Allow your next inhalation to be a little
bit longer and deeper than your last one. Let
your exhalation be a little bit slower and more
complete than the last one.

With each successive breath, let your inhalation be longer, fuller, and deeper than the last . . . Your exhalation slower, smoother, and more complete. Do this until you are breathing in completely, to your full capacity . . . And breathing out slowly, until you have emptied your lungs of all their air.

Now let your breathing return to a natural rhythm, perhaps a bit deeper and fuller than usual . . . Feel energy come in with each inhalation, and tension flow out with each exhalation. Your thoughts are turned inward and you feel at ease. Clear your mind of all thoughts . . . Let your mind be empty and clear.

Into that quiet space of your mind, slowly form the picture of a calm, quiet pond of water.

See the water reflecting the blue sky above . . . Notice how smooth and still the surface of the pond is . . . Around the pond, you can see a forest of trees completely surrounding the water . . . Green grass and bushes are growing to the edge of the pond . . . Cattails and lily pads are growing out of the water here and there near the banks.

Allow yourself to flow into this quiet space with each breath you take . . . Float quietly into this scene just as the white clouds float quietly through the blue sky above the pond.

Begin to look at this place from many different angles. See it from the level of the water itself, as though through the eyes of a frog . . . See it from the branches of the trees, like a squirrel might . . . Soar high above it all, and see it through the eyes of a hawk.

Notice how the pond and woods are teeming with life . . . Hear the sounds of humming insects and singing birds . . . Hear the rush of the wind through the leaves and branches . . . Smell the scents of the flowers that bloom on the shoreline.

At every aspect of the scene fellow creatures are fully engaged in the process of living.

Feel the connection to those creatures that Native Americans call "All Our Relations." You might see a raccoon coming down from a tree to hunt around the pond's edge . . . You might notice a fish pluck an insect off the surface of the pond . . . In the cattails you might see a bird building a nest . . . Take time to explore the pond and see your fellow creatures move through this scene, and as you do this, allow yourself to be drawn to one of the living creatures in your scene. Follow this creature. Prepare to become one with it.

Pause for 10 seconds

When you have found a creature that you feel close to, begin to see the world through its eyes . . . Explore the pond as though the camera of your mind was focusing through the lenses of the creature's eyes. Begin to feel movement through its body. Feel its wings, fins, or legs become your own.

If you are an insect, you can now see all around you, not just in front. If you are a mammal, your sense of smell is so much sharper and tells you so much more about the world around you. And with any creature, your hearing is most likely more acute.

Slow down. Your perception of time is entirely different. Allow yourself to move through "a day in the life" of this creature.

If your creature is active during the night, then spend your time visualizing it at night. See yourself walking, swimming, crawling, flying, or hopping through the darkness. Explore your territory . . . hunt for food, and play.

Be your animal . . . Be your animal as it moves.

Pause for 1 minute

Now begin to experience the part of the day or night that you, as this creature, are not active . . . See yourself being still or sleeping.

Now slowly move out of being that creature and see yourself again, in the form of your own body, standing by the pond.

Tune in to all your own senses and feel, taste, touch, see, hear, and smell. Experience your surroundings completely . . .

Explore . . . Play . . . Rest and relax.

Forage for something to eat, climb a tree, or swim in the pond. Do whatever comes naturally to you . . . Enjoy your day.

Pause for 1 minute

Slowly allow your day to come to a close.

Pause for 10 seconds

Now start preparing to leave the pond . . . Take a careful look around . . . Listen to the sounds of this place . . . Look for the creature whose form you took earlier . . . Say goodbye to it and to this place.

Feel the earth that supports you underneath your back, even if you are on a floor some distance from the surface of the earth . . . Acknowledge your connection to the earth that completely sustains you.

Allow yourself to remain grounded with the

energy of the earth, energized by the breath of
the life-giving air that surrounds you, and
warmed by the sun that shines down on us all.

Become aware of your breath again and breathe
in deeply . . . Feel the energy flow in with that
breath . . . You might like to stretch as you
breathe in fully. Slowly allow yourself to become
aware of the space you are in . . . Quietly,
gently, allow your eyelids to open.

Repeat the above instructions until everyone is alert.

The Beach

Walt Schafer

Time: 5 minutes

In this script, participants imagine they are on vacation, strolling along a quiet ocean beach, free of the usual daily pressures and hassles.

Script

Prepare yourself for the experience by getting comfortable in a reclining or sitting position, preferably in a quiet place.

Take in a long, deep breath . . . Hold it . . . Now slowly and completely exhale. Allow your jaw and shoulders to drop as you exhale.

Visualize the following, allowing your mind to roam freely in its own way.

Imagine you are on vacation. No cares, no worries. You feel completely free from your usual daily pressures and hassles.

You are walking along the water's edge on a quiet, secluded, warm ocean beach . . . You are dressed comfortably and are either alone or with someone close to you, whichever you prefer. As you stroll along the water's edge, you feel the coolness of the damp sand under your feet . . . and hear the gentle rolling of the waves . . . Under your arm you carry a rolled-up towel.

You turn away from the water and look at the soft, white warm sand. You pick a spot where you can be alone and still . . . You put down your towel, and using it as a pillow, you lie down on the soft, pleasantly warm sand.

You feel the warmth of the sand on your back, your legs, and your arms.

You notice the deep blue of the late morning sky. It is completely clear, except for one wispy cloud near the horizon over the water.

You feel the gentle warmth of the sand beneath . . . You feel utterly relaxed and still. For the next several minutes, continue to experience this place, allowing your mind to wander as it wishes. Enjoy this very pleasant sensation of stillness, warmth, and quiet.

Pause for 2 minutes

And now imagine getting up . . . gathering up your towel . . . walking back to the water's edge . . . Again, you experience the cool, damp, sand underfoot . . . You continue on along the beach, feeling alert, refreshed, peaceful, and renewed. You give yourself credit for this positive experience.

Now bring your attention back to the present. Draw a deep breath. Open your eyes.

Repeat the above instructions until everyone is alert.

Reprinted with author's permission from *Stress Management for Wellness, Second Edition,* Fort Worth: Harcourt, Brace and Jovanovich.

Flying with the Eagle

Maggie Zadikov

Time: 15 minutes

In this script for kids (and for the young-at-heart), participants leave their homes through a secret door, travel to the forest of a magnificent Mother Eagle, and go for a ride on her back.

Script

Imagine that you are lying comfortably and safely in bed at home. Close your eyes . . . Stretch out your arms and legs . . . Take in a nice, big breath of air . . . and let the air go all the way out. It's time to be a little quiet for a while.

Imagine that a skylight or window is over your bed, and through it you can feel the rays of the sun shining down on you . . . The sky is clear and blue, and you feel the warmth of the sun beating down on your head, warming and relaxing your face and neck . . . shoulders, arms, chest . . . hips, thighs, knees . . . lower legs, ankles, and feet. You are feeling very relaxed, and very comfortable in your bed.

In your mind, get up and walk to the other side of the room and open the door of your

closet . . . You notice a secret door at the back of
your closet. Even though you've never seen it
before, it looks like it could lead to something
fun. You open the secret door and go through it.
You come to a flight of stairs and you walk
down . . . down . . . down . . . down the stairs.

You then step onto a dirt path and head
towards the shore of a lake.

Smell the fragrance of pine trees as you stroll
along the dirt path. Look at the color of the lake
water and the sun sparkling on it.

At the lake is a rowboat. You climb in and feel
yourself settle on some soft, colorful
cushions . . . The rowboat starts crossing the
lake as if by magic . . . slish-slosh, slish-slosh,
slish-slosh.

Eventually, you get to the other side of the lake
and the rowboat gently stops . . . See yourself
getting out of the boat and stepping onto the
shore.

A grassy meadow, strewn with blue . . .
red . . . yellow . . . orange . . . and purple
wildflowers, spreads out before you. Take in a
nice big breath and smell the flowers.

You pass through the meadow and come to the

edge of a forest. You decide to explore it and see what you might see.

The trees in the forest look tall and friendly . . . The air smells clean and crisp. It's a friendly forest and it makes you feel safe and happy. Explore it.

Soon you come to a tree that has branches at just the right height for climbing, and you decide to climb this tree. You grab onto the first branch, and reach for the next, and the next, and the next.

You climb up the tree higher and higher, and right as you get near the very top, you notice a bird's nest. It's a rather large nest, and as you look carefully, you notice that there are several little birds in it.

Take a good look at the birds and count how many birds you see . . . As you are counting, you suddenly see a large shadow darkening the area above you. You look up and see that the Mother bird has returned. And she's a beautiful Bald Eagle.

She lights on one of the branches just above you and starts to talk to you. She says, "I see you have found my nest and you are looking at my little ones."

You nod your head and say, "Yes" . . . Then she continues, "Would you like to go for a ride on my back?"

And you say, "Oh yes I would, but how can I do that?" She says, "First you have to shrink a little. Just close your eyes and count to three." So you do that. You close your eyes and you hear yourself say, "one, two, three." And as you say the number three, your stomach feels a little funny and you feel a little different.

You open your eyes and you watch yourself shrink, smaller and smaller and smaller, until you are no bigger than the size of the little eaglets in the nest . . . Shrinking feels good and you feel happy.

The Mother Eagle then tells you to climb onto her back, to scurry up right behind her neck, and to hold onto her feathers. She asks, "Are you ready?" And you say excitedly, "Yes." You hear the eaglets start to chirp as she spreads her wings and begins to slowly rise into the sky.

You soar above the trees as she gracefully flies through the sky above the forest.

As you are flying, look down and see the meadow with the little wild flowers . . . See the lake with the rowboat on its shore.

Slowly and smoothly, the Mother Eagle carries
you higher and higher and into the sky. You feel
the wind on your skin . . . It's wonderful to be
flying in the air, free as the eagle, looking down
over familiar territory. Why you can even see
your own house far below!

You keep on flying in great big circles . . . This
way and that way . . . The eagle soars and then
gently glides without moving her wings. She lets
the wind carry both of you for a moment.

Finally, she begins to descend towards the
forest . . . The tops of the trees get closer and
closer . . . She finds her tree and slowly comes
to land on the branch closest to the nest. She
asks you to carefully climb off her back and on
to the branch.

Then the Mother Eagle asks you to once again
close your eyes and count backwards from three
to one. So you count, "Three, two, one." And
once again you feel that funny little feeling in
the pit of your stomach and you feel your body
begin to grow.

You get bigger and bigger and bigger . . . You
open up your eyes and you are once again your
normal size. You thank the eagle for the
wonderful ride up in the sky and you say
goodbye to the little eagles.

Slowly and carefully you climb back down, limb by limb, to the bottom of the tree.

You find your way out of the forest and hike through the meadow, feeling the soft grass under your feet and smelling the fragrance of the wild flowers as you move along.

You come to the lake and see the little rowboat waiting for you. Once again you step into the rowboat and lay down on the soft cushions. You feel the boat begin to move smoothly across the lake.

The boat gradually comes to halt at the other side. You stand up, step out of the boat, and begin trekking up the dirt path and through the grove of pine trees with their wonderful fresh smell.

You come to the stairway and you climb up . . . up . . . up . . . up, and up the steps until you get to the secret door at the back of your closet.

You open the door, step through it, and then shut it. You walk through the closet and across your room to your bed. You sit back down on the bed and remember how many little eagles you counted in the nest.

You lie back down thinking about your exciting ride on the eagle's back.

The End.

Stretch your arms and legs and open your eyes.

Repeat the above instruction until everyone is alert.

Oak Creek

Tom Tapin and his sister Julie Lusk

Time: 10 minutes

In this script, participants experience and feel a personal connection with the energy and the healing power of the earth and sky.

Script

Imagine that you are walking through a meadow . . . a meadow in the Southwest . . . a meadow with deep, washed-out colors. Notice the path underfoot . . . feel what it is like . . . hear the sounds as you take each step, one by one . . . Looking around, you see a field to one side . . . and a wide creek on the other.

As you continue walking, become aware of the sun shining on you . . . feel its radiance . . . its warmth . . . its heat . . . You feel warm all over . . .the heat is gentle . . . and welcoming. It gives you a feeling of being at home.

As you look to one side, you begin to pay attention to the water in the creek . . . Hear the sounds the water makes . . . See the water . . . Feel yourself walking over to it . . . step by step . . . feeling the ground beneath your feet.

Standing beside the creek, you kick off your shoes and step into the water and feel its coolness against your skin ... The water surrounds your feet. Sink your feet and toes into the sandy creek bottom.

Feel the water's wetness and its coolness. Feel your connection to the earth through your feet ... Wiggle your toes ... Feel the earth's power ... the energy ... Now feel the water line around your ankles ... Feel the water line ... Feel the energy and power beneath your feet.

Now let the feeling of the earth's energy come up from your feet to your calves ... from your feet to your calves to your knees ... from your feet through your legs to your hips and torso ... from your hips and torso past your heart and all the way to your shoulders ... Now it moves down your arms to your fingertips ... and back up your arms to your shoulders ... neck, face, and head.

Feel the energy going all the way back down your body ... slowly and easily ... to the water and earth ... and back up again ... Feel the energy flowing all around.

Once again, let the energy come from the earth and up through your body ... like a fountain ... sprinkling the energy through the

top of your head and showering you all
over . . . sprinkling you with earth energy.

Now look at the water . . . See the sparkles . . .
the reflections . . . Watch the water as it passes
by . . . Feel and see the movement . . . Hear it.

Look up the creek and watch the water flow past
you . . . Realize where the water has been and
where it is going as it circles the entire earth . . .
and be part of it.

Looking up, you see the trees and the leaves
blowing in the breeze . . . Now pick out one tree
and gaze upon it . . . Notice its size . . . its
age . . . See its branches and leaves . . . Look up
overhead and see the sky . . . its magnificent
color . . . its beautiful clouds.

Now feel the energy from the sky traveling
down from the heavens, through the top of your
head . . . through your heart and down to your
feet . . . across the earth and up to your tree . . .
back from your tree . . . across the earth . . .
through your feet . . . legs . . . torso . . .
heart . . . head and back up to the sky . . . Feel
the flow of energy.

Feeling your connection with the heavens . . .
take it all in . . . soak it up . . .

Pause for 1 minute

Draw your attention back to standing in the creek . . . step by step, walk out of the water . . . put your shoes on . . . and now walk back down the path . . . and through the meadow. Notice how refreshed and grounded you are.

Take a full deep breath . . . all the way in . . . slow and easy . . . and all the way out . . . Each time you breathe, you feel more and more alive . . . more and more alert.

Pause

When you are ready . . . begin to stretch and move . . . and open your eyes.

Repeat the above instructions until everyone is alert.

The Night Sky

Don Tubesing

Time: 8 minutes

In this script, participants imagine looking at the stars of a clear night sky and feeling their minds expand into the infinite expanse of space.

Script

As you relax yourself . . . and prepare to enjoy the wide expanse of the night sky . . . Begin to close your eyes . . . and let go.

Notice any part of your body . . . that feels constricted and small . . . As you breathe out . . . let this area relax . . . Feel yourself open . . . and expand . . . as you let go of the tension.

Once again . . . Allow yourself to expand, as you breathe in . . . and to relax as you breathe out.

Imagine that you are looking up at the night sky. You are outside . . . away from the lights. The night is clear . . . and calm. The stars are shining . . . The evening holds a quiet magic.

You notice where you are . . .

You notice the season of the year . . .

You are alone . . . but safe and calm . . . in the quiet of the night.

You are quiet . . . filled with a sense of awe . . . as you gaze on the expanse of the night.

You notice the brilliant diamond lights . . . that blanket the heavens.

You notice a layering of the expanse . . . stars that puncture the darkness with clarity . . . others that dim . . . still others only subliminal suggestions. Mere hints of the thousands and millions of stars not seen . . . that extend into the infinite expanse . . . which your eyes cannot reach.

You look over the whole sky . . . and you notice what you see . . . as you look . . . from horizon . . . to horizon.

You focus on a cluster of stars . . . Stars appear . . . at the edge of your vision. You focus on them . . . But they disappear as you do.

Your eyes wander . . . a falling star streaks across the darkness . . . And before you get focused . . . it disappears and vaporizes into a

memory . . . a memory that touched you . . . a
memory that you never got hold of.

Your eyes focus on stars that sparkle . . . on
stars that remain constant . . . on stars that come
in and out of focus . . . seeming to disappear,
then reappear at will.

Your eyes come to rest . . . You focus on
nothing . . . But you take in the sense of the
whole . . . And you feel the expanse . . . You
sense the unlimited infinite . . . without known
boundaries . . . that goes on forever.

And you breathe . . . deeply . . . Taking this
expanse into yourself . . . fully.

You let go of your own boundaries . . . you
expand into the night sky . . . you live for the
moment in the wonder of the sky.

And you let go of your boundaries . . .
connected with awe . . . to the expanse . . . that
always holds more than you can see . . . that
seems to be bigger than your imagination.

And you awe . . . at the sky . . . which goes on
without ending . . . of which you are a part.

And you allow yourself . . . to fill . . . to
expand . . . with the wonder of the moment.

Pause

When you are ready . . . you allow yourself to return . . . from this vision. Still open . . . unconstrained . . . relaxed . . . having been expanded . . . having been touched . . . by the infinite expanse of the clear night sky . . . that extends out forever.

Repeat the above instructions until everyone is alert.

Ocean Waves

Debbie Stevens

Time: 12 minutes

In this script, participants dissolve their worries and troubles by imagining they are listening to the rhythm of the ocean waves.

Script

Lean back. Let your eyes gently close. At this time, you don't have a care in the world. You feel totally relaxed . . . Breathe in and out . . . Aaaaah! Feel the breath as it leaves your body.

Focus your attention on your breath. Take in a deep breath, allowing your body to fill up with air as if it were a balloon . . . Hold the breath a moment, then allow yourself to slowly release all the air as if your body were a balloon deflating.

Feel the relaxation overcome your body as you exhale . . . With each breath you feel more and more relaxed.

Imagine that you are walking on a beach . . . The warm grains of sand gently tickle your feet as you stroll along . . . Around you are sea oats waving their long-stemmed bodies in the ocean breeze . . . Overhead you see more birds flying through the sky . . . Listen to the sounds of the birds.

Your feet carry you to a place where you can sit comfortably and face the vast ocean. With that expanse of water before you, you breathe deeply in and out. You are very relaxed.

You feel the constant sea breeze touching every part of your skin and hair, taking away the sting from the sun's constant rays. The air wraps around you, like a blanket, protecting you from the cool dampness of the beach.

You smell the salt of the ocean water and think about the sea life fed by this great body of water. Imagine the animal and plant life supported by the ocean.

Let yourself go in the enormity of the ocean stretching before you and to both sides of you as far as you can see.

Focus your attention on the ocean before you . . . Hear the waves as they crash onto the shore near where you sit. You are aware of the powerful life-force of the ocean.

See how each wave builds to a crest, then falls onto the shore, becoming little bubbles of foam on the beach, leaving its watermark on the sand before retreating to that great body of water to begin the cycle once again.

Allow yourself to watch the waves as they form and fall, retreat, and form and fall again. Fill your mind only with the rhythm of the ocean.

Pause for 2 minutes

Focus your attention on the waves as they rise and fall before you. Let the persistent motion of the waves fill your mind.

Relax. You don't have to go anywhere or do anything. Simply enjoy the clear, blue sky above, the sand beneath you, and the ocean beyond. Let the waves, the rhythm with which they pound the shore, mesmerize you. Be aware of nothing else, only the calming rhythm of the ocean.

Pause for 2 minutes

Be aware of the present, of what is now, of the coming and going of each wave as the coming and going of each moment. Pay attention to the coming and going of each ocean wave.

With the green sea in front of you and the blue sky above, realize that you are as small as a grain of sand in the ocean of the universe. All worries and cares seem insignificant compared

77

to this vast, peaceful universe around you. Feel the peacefulness around you. Breathe it in with the ocean air . . . Feel the calmness of the ocean in its constant rhythm.

You are very relaxed, at peace with yourself and with the universe around you. Take the cool calm of the ocean with you.

Feeling refreshed, you find yourself leaving the ocean behind. You find yourself walking away from the beach, heading back home.

Pause

Bring your awareness to the present . . .
Silently, count backwards from 5 to 1. On the count of 1, stretch, slowly breathe in and out, then open your eyes feeling alert and calm.

Repeat the above instructions until everyone is alert.

Inner Answers

Taking the time to regularly explore and reflect upon the inner world of intuition, feelings, and thoughts can be uplifting and is a sure path to personal, emotional, mental, and spiritual growth.

The guided meditations in this section help people get in touch with their intuitive inner selves so that they may find answers to life's questions from within.

Your Inner Advisor

Bob Fellows

Time: 18 minutes

In this meditation, participants have a conversation with their inner advisor to develop their intuition—making decisions based on gut feelings rather than on reactions to social influence.

After you've led this visualization, you may help participants process their experience by asking the following questions. What was your fantasy place like? And what does that mean? What did it mean for you to have this particular advisor? What did you think of to ask the advisor, and why? What did the advisor's answers mean? What part of it is true for you?

Note: You may want to use a relaxation exercise prior to this visualization.

Script

Close your eyes ... Allow yourself to relax physically ... mentally ... emotionally ... and spiritually ... Feel your feet and legs ... your back ... abdomen, and chest relax ... Feel your hands ... arms ... shoulders ... neck ... face ... and head relax ... Continue to relax more and more using whatever method you're familiar with to become as comfortable as possible.

Now imagine a place where you feel calm and
inspired ... a place that you like ... It may be
a place where you have been ... where you
have gained some insight ... or a place that
you make up ... Or a combination ... You
may imagine a house, the hollow trunk of a tree,
a meadow, or a place by the sea ... You can
change my instructions to fit your special
place ... Allow the details of this special place
to occur slowly and naturally to you ... Permit
yourself to be surprised by what you discover at
this special place.

Imagine some kind of path leading to your
special place ... See or feel yourself walking
along this path ... getting closer and closer to
your special place ... Notice as many details as
you can ... Is the place big or small? ... light
or dark? ... Have people been there ... or is it
undisturbed?

When you get to your special place, enter it in
any way you like, and look around ... Pick part
of it to be your own personal and private
place ... You may put whatever you would like
to have here to feel comfortable.

You might have a couple of chairs so that two
people could sit down and have a conversation.
You can also have books, pictures, or objects that
are sources of wisdom for you ... or you can
have nothing if you wish.

In a few moments, you're going to meet your
Inner Advisor . . . This is a something or
someone who is very wise . . . who cares about
you deeply . . . but who does not take authority
away from you. When your advisor suggests an
action to you, you're ultimately the one who
decides what you're going to do.

Instead of planning ahead about who your Inner
Advisor is going to be, let yourself be
surprised . . . Your Inner Advisor can be a
person, man or woman . . . young or old . . .
someone who really exists or existed . . .
someone you make up . . . or a combination . . .
You may even have an Inner Advisor that is not
even a person, maybe an animal . . . a fantasy
creature . . . or even a mood.

I'd like you to meet your advisor slowly so that
you can notice details about your advisor as you
are approached.

Get ready now to discover your Inner Advisor.

Notice that your Inner Advisor is a pinpoint, far
off in the distance and is now ready to begin
approaching you . . . With your own will, bring
your Inner Advisor closer . . . You're the one
who's in charge when your Inner Advisor comes
to you . . . Watch as your Inner Advisor
transforms . . . growing from a pinpoint . . .
becoming larger and larger . . . you can stop

your advisor at any time to notice details and find answers to questions such as, "Is your Inner Advisor male or female . . . old or young . . . big or small? . . . What is your Inner Advisor wearing? . . . What is the expression on the face? . . . Do you know this person?"

Notice the hands and any other details that will help you to gain insight into your advisor . . . Continue bringing your advisor in closer, going at your own pace until finally the Advisor comes into your space . . . Invite your Inner Advisor into your special place.

Greet your Inner Advisor with a hug or a handshake or a hello, whatever seems appropriate . . . You can begin your conversation anytime you wish . . . You can communicate in any way you want with your Inner Advisor, with or without words.

In your first meeting, you may just talk with your Inner Advisor about what you want your advisor to do for you. Remember, you're in charge. Your Inner Advisor can remember things for you that you forget during the day . . . give you wise advice and new ideas . . . and help you make decisions that are difficult for you.

You may ask your Inner Advisor specific questions . . . Let yourself be surprised by the answers you receive . . . Your advisor may not always tell you what you want to hear, but will tell you what you need to hear.

If your Inner Advisor is a person you know in real life, then, in this space, this version can be even more wise and more caring than the person is in real life.

Remember, even though you let yourself be surprised by the answers your Inner Advisor gives you, you're still in charge . . . It is up to you to decide how you will act on whatever advice you receive.

Pause for 2 minutes

When you are ready to end your conversation with your Inner Advisor, get up and say goodbye in any way that seems right . . . Your advisor will leave and go off into the distance . . . Remember that you can see, feel or hear your advisor again whenever you want by doing this exercise . . . You may have a different Inner Advisor next time. That's OK too.

If you want, you can stay in your space for a while and meditate on your experience with your Inner Advisor . . . or on what you would like to do about any decisions that you are making.

Pause

When you're ready, you can leave your special place . . . Close the door behind you . . . see or feel yourself walk away . . . and finally . . . picture yourself in the place where you started this exercise . . . and open your eyes.

Repeat the above instructions until everyone is alert.

Fortune Cookies

Richard Boyum

Time: 20 minutes

In this visualization, participants tap into their intuitive selves by imagining that they are reading messages contained in fortune cookies.

After you've led this exercise, you can help the participants process their experience by asking them to write down what they saw in their fortune cookies. Ask them to share the insights and implications of what their cookies had to say.

Script

Allow yourself to get into a very comfortable position . . . Now close your eyes . . . Let your eyes rest . . . Closing your eyes will allow your imagination, your inner eye, to open up and become active . . . Wiggle and move around until you feel relaxed and comfortable . . . settling down.

Imagine that you are sitting at a table in a Chinese restaurant after eating your favorite meal . . . The meal was delicious and satisfying . . . Look around the restaurant . . . See the patterns on the dishes . . . the tablecloth . . . the walls.

As you are looking around, you notice your server coming towards your table ... carrying a large lacquered bowl. The beautiful bowl is filled with fortune cookies ... Watch as she places the bowl before you ... Imagine yourself reaching into the bowl and mixing up the cookies with your fingers ... Feel the texture of the cookies as you touch them ... Hear the sound the cookies make as you gently mix them up.

Imagine picking up a fortune cookie ... Notice its shape ... Be aware of how it feels as you hold it in your hand ... Just hold it without opening it up.

In this first fortune cookie, you will find a phrase, a word, a sentence, or possibly even a picture or visual image of something positive that you need to see ... or hear ... about yourself right now ... Maybe it is something you have not recognized or that you have not thought about for awhile.

Now, if you wish, you can open up the fortune cookie ... Pull out the piece of paper with the message on it ... and look at it carefully ... Read what it says ... Later on you will be asked to write your message down and think about it once again.

Pause for 20 seconds

Now reach back into the bowl and pick out another cookie . . . This second cookie relates to an issue that you need to work on at this time in your life . . . Again, this may be a word, a phrase, a sentence, or a picture . . . Before you open the cookie and see what is there, take a moment to think about an issue that you need to work on.

Now open the cookie . . . Let the message come to you rather than forcing it . . . Let it just happen.

Pause for 20 seconds

Now please reach into the bowl for the third cookie . . . This cookie contains something you need to say to someone . . . It may be something positive or it may relate to an issue that is causing conflict . . . This cookie will tell you what you need to say.

Now, if you wish, you may open up the cookie and again look for the phrase, picture, sentence, or word that will tell you what you need to know . . . Take a few moments to reflect on this . . . something you need to say to someone.

Pause for 20 seconds

Now pick out another fortune cookie from the bowl . . . Hold this cookie in your hand and wait until I suggest when to open it . . . In this

cookie, you will find the opposite of what was in
the previous cookie . . . In other words, if in the
previous cookie you saw something positive to
communicate to someone, in this cookie, you
will find something that you need to
communicate that is more difficult for you,
something that you have been putting off . . .
For example, it may be a conflict that is keeping
one of your relationships from being as trusting,
as honest, or as intimate as you want it to be.

If, in the previous cookie, you thought of
something difficult to communicate, then find
something positive to communicate from this
new cookie . . . If you would like to see what is
in this cookie, you may open it up now.

Pause for 20 seconds

Once again, take another fortune cookie from
the bowl . . . Hold it in your hand . . . Now put
it in an imaginary pocket . . . Know that there is
an extremely important message in it . . . I have
no idea what that message is.

Please don't open this cookie for at least twenty-
four hours. When enough time has gone by and
you feel ready to open it, you will find that it
contains an insight that is very important to you.

Now spend a few moments looking over the
special messages from your fortune cookies.

Realize that these messages are the most important ones you could have right now.

Pause for 10 seconds

Begin to bring your attention back to this room . . . begin stretching and moving . . . allow yourself to feel alert . . . When ready, open your eyes.

Repeat the above instructions until everyone is alert.

Your Inner Child

Judy Fulop

Time: 15 minutes

In this script, participants get to know, communicate with, and learn from their inner child.

Script

Allow yourself to imagine your favorite scenic place . . . This place can be the seashore . . . the mountains . . . your backyard . . . your house . . . wherever you feel most comfortable and can spend time . . . even if the world is calling you to come back . . . Allow yourself to walk towards this place.

What do you see around you? . . . Continue moving towards your special place . . . As you get closer, begin to notice the faint outline of a child sitting . . . or standing in your favorite place . . . As you come closer, notice that this child looks like you . . . but a younger, smaller version of you . . . Notice what your child looks like . . . What is he or she doing?

Is your child taking in the sights . . . or looking at the ground? . . . As you get closer, reach out to your child and say hello in whatever way you

think your child would want to be greeted . . .
Ask your child if you can spend some time
together.

If your child does not want you to get too
close . . . respect your child's need for distance
and just be with your child from a distance . . .
If your child allows . . . go over and sit, or
stand, behind your child . . . Look in the same
direction as your child . . . as if you were
one . . . See what your child sees . . . Hear what
your child hears . . . Feel what your child feels.

Ask your child what it is like to be a small
child . . . and what is good about life . . . What
concerns does your child have? . . . Keep in
mind that no concern is too small . . . or too
large . . . Listen with an open mind.

Then ask your child what he or she most wants
or needs from you . . . Allow your child to
communicate in his or her own way. He or she
may point . . . draw a picture . . . or
whatever . . . Your child may just want to be
held . . . told a story . . . or be given something.

Allow your child time to think and then answer
you in whatever way is unique to your child . . .
What does he or she most need or want from
you?

Listen to . . . look at . . . think about what your
child most wants from you . . . If you can, go
ahead and give it to your child . . . If it is
something that you cannot give, tell your child
what you can give . . . If it is something that is
possible in the future, tell your child when this
will be possible and give your child something
symbolic of your promise for the future.

Give your child a hug . . . and ask your child if
he or she wants to go back with you today . . . If
so, allow your child to say goodbye to his or her
surroundings, with the promise to return
whenever your child desires.

If your child does not want to come with
you . . . tell your child you will return when he
or she calls for you . . . If you want, tell your
child that someday . . . you would like for
both of you to be together.

Pause

Now it is time to bring your attention back to
the present.

Begin to picture this room . . . When you are
ready . . . take a few deep breaths . . . stretch
out . . . and open your eyes.

Repeat the above instructions until everyone is alert.

Time Travel: So What Do You Want to Do for A Living?

John Zach

Time: 20 minutes

In this script, participants imagine the future to discover potential career paths and living conditions.

Note: You may want to use a relaxation exercise prior to this visualization.

Script

Listen to my voice and begin feeling relaxed and comfortable . . . You are going to take an imaginary trip. You are going to travel to a place where you would like to be living . . . to a job you would like to be working at in the future. Let your imagination go into the future 5–10–15 years or more . . . I am not sure how many years you will imagine, but I am sure you have the ability and information to project yourself sometime into the future.

The way in which you explore your future will be unique to you. Some people are better at visualizing the future, others at hearing or feeling it, but I am sure that you will be able to effectively use one, two, or all of your senses to really experience this future life, to really learn about yourself and what you value in life.

As you become aware of the many sensory experiences, you will become more relaxed and comfortable, for there is no place you need to go. When your body feels more and more relaxed, your mind will feel wide awake and involved with this experience . . . So relax and be open to what you are seeing, feeling, and hearing.

Now imagine that you are traveling by some type of transportation to a place where you would like to live.

What type of transportation are you using?

What does it look like? What does it sound like? . . . What does it smell like?

How does this transportation represent who you are as a person? . . . How do you feel when you're in it?

Are there other people around you or are you alone?

As you travel along, look at the scenery of the country you're in . . . As you come to the place where you want to live, notice whether it is in a rural or urban area.

What do you like about this area? ... See it ... hear it ... smell it.

What is the environment like? Is it crowded? ... clean? ... What is the climate like?

Are there any other people around?

You arrive at the place where you want to live.

What does it look like? ... Is it a house or apartment ... How big is it? ... What is the place made out of?

Now go inside. Is there anybody in there? ... Look around and notice what your lifestyle is like. Is it expensive or modest? ... What do you like about this place and how do you feel?

As you look around and become aware of what your place is like, you notice a number of special objects that are connected to your past ... objects that have great meaning to you and to what you are as a person.

As you notice these things, allow yourself to experience them with your different senses.

Pause after each of the following items to allow ample time for participants to use their imagination.

One of your favorite books is on the table.

On top of the TV is one of the most important movies you have ever seen.

Hanging on the walls are pictures of your best friend, people whom you care about and who love you, and the most important teacher in your life.

Your favorite piece of music is playing on the stereo.

On the floor is one of your favorite childhood toys.

And behind the toy is the gift that you most value.

Why is this gift so valuable to you?

How have these objects helped you develop into the person you are now? . . . How have they affected your value structure?

You become aware again of your new place . . . and of you being there. Then, in the quiet, you notice that your telephone is ringing.

You answer the phone and hear the voice of a very good friend . . . You feel comforted to hear from this friend.

Your friend has heard of your move and your new job and begins to ask you questions. As you hear yourself answering your friend's questions, you will gain a better insight and understanding of your new job.

"What type of work are you doing?" your friend asks.

"Where do you work?"

"What is the environment like?"

"What time does your work day begin and end? ... How many hours a week do you work?"

"What does your place of work look like? ... Are you around many people or mostly by yourself?"

"Do you work with people ... data ... machines ... or a combination?"

"What is an average day like?"

"What are the possibilities of advancement?"

"How much money do you make? Is it enough?"

"What are some things you like about your work?"

"How do you feel?"

Your friend hangs up and you feel happy and relaxed.

Now think about what your new job would be like . . . How does it match with what you value in life and in people? . . . What has this experience taught you about who you are and what you want in life?

Pause

Now prepare to come back to the here and now, remembering the things you thought and felt during this imaginary trip. Open your eyes and stretch out, feeling rested and alert.

Repeat the above instructions until everyone is alert.

Healing

Integrating the mind, body, emotions, and spirit opens up vast inner resources of intuition, wisdom, and personal power.

So many of us live as if fragmented—thinking of one thing, saying something else, acting one way publicly, while feelings, moods, and emotions provide a constantly changing and inconsistent undertow.

The guided meditations in this section focus on using the mind to heal the body and emotions and to bring thoughts, words, actions, and feelings into harmony and alignment.

Love, Joy, and Optimism

Bernie Siegel

Time: 30 minutes

In this guided meditation, participants journey down a private path; encounter their own personal guide and shadow; feel love, joy, hope, and optimism; and learn to accept themselves no matter what is going on in their lives.

Note: Choose some type of relaxing music as a background for this script.

Script

Let the music fill you with a sense of tranquility. Let it carry you gently to that meditative place where you can use all of your senses—visual, tactile, auditory, and olfactory— to make the imagery more powerful for you.

So now let's take a moment, a moment that you're entitled to . . . and start on a journey to those places where you will feel like celebrating. Let love . . . joy . . . hope . . . and optimism enter your life.

Take a moment . . . to breathe in love . . . breathe in joy . . . breathe in hope . . . breathe in optimism.

Love, joy, and hope are real ... They are all
available to you ... Notice what these qualities
do to your body ... and your mind ... as you
breathe them in.

And when you breathe out ... let go ... Let
the tension go ... Relax the jaw muscles ...
Rest your eyelids ... and let them close ... Let
the back and neck muscles be loved ... They
carry a burden ... But let the burden roll off
your shoulders.

Breathe with your chest and your
diaphragm ... Don't let anything restrict those
muscles as they move deeply ... and let the
movement and the love move down through
your body ... move each part ... be aware of
it ... love it ... and relax it.

What are you striving for? Reaching for?

Let go of the opposite of what you are reaching
for ... Let go of the pain ... Let go of the
sadness ... Let go of the despair ... the
resentment ... the hatred ... Let go.

You can't free yourself ... from anyone or
anything ... until you allow love ... joy ...
hope, and optimism to fill your life ... And so
take a deep breath ... And allow yourself to
settle down.

Just feel the peace filling your life and your
body ... and how that relaxes you ... Just
settle down.

Just watch the color ... and the feelings move
through your body ... relaxing the muscles ...
relieving discomfort ... Give an extra measure
of love to every part of your body that is having
difficulty of one kind or another ... You can
love yourself well ... We are all lovers ... We
are not killers ... Just love yourself ... until
you are filled with love.

Make sure that every cell is open to that
love ... And see any problems being breathed
out or eliminated in a way that is comfortable for
you ... And take a moment ... to purify and
cleanse ... your mind and body ... in a way
that feels right for you.

And now we are ready ... Ready for a
beautiful trip ... A trip to a land that is filled
with love and creative energy, joy, and hope ...
And you are the creator ... You are to create
your ideal universe.

If you were the creator ... what would you put
into your corner of the universe? ... What
would you let every flower know? ... Every
blade of grass? ... Every butterfly? ... Every
animal ... Every bird ... Every cloud ... the
sun ... the moon, the stars.

106

It's all up to you . . . There's a giant easel in front of you . . . Paint your picture . . . Create your world.

You are directing . . . It's your movie . . . in your mind . . . Create it . . . and step into your world . . . Totally safe . . . Feel the love . . . This is your garden of Eden . . . Feel the joy . . . The potential . . . The future . . . You are directing your universe . . . There are no limits.

Take a moment here to just absorb . . . a feeling that you may never have felt before . . . Total love . . . total acceptance . . . total joy . . . total hope.

Here hope is a memory of the future. And this place exists forever as a part of the universe that others experience . . . And you can always come here . . . because the bridge that you build . . . connects it to the universe and to your path . . . There is two-way traffic on that bridge . . . If the universe gets difficult . . . cross to your corner of the universe . . . to restore yourself.

And as you cross your bridge . . . you'll notice beautiful, loving light . . . shining ahead of you on your path . . . And coming out of that light, a figure will be walking towards you.

You may already see one . . . or one may appear in a few moments . . . And as this figure comes closer . . . you will know perhaps who it is.

And if not . . . when the figure is close enough, ask for his or her name . . . And know . . . that this person represents an inner guide for you . . . Someone who will guide you and help you on your journey.

If no one appeared at this moment . . . you might turn and notice that the light has created a shadow . . . And by looking into your shadow, you can be helped too.

Often . . . talking to our dark side is as meaningful and filled with guidance . . . as talking to the light.

Now, take your guide, or your shadow . . . and move forward on your path and your journey . . . allowing your feelings . . . and their guidance and light . . . to help you make right turns . . . and right decisions . . . and right choices . . . to lead you towards love and hope and joy.

Ahead of you, you will notice . . . that your path leads through a tunnel in a mountain . . . And if you look through the tunnel . . . you will

see a speck of light where it comes out on the
other side . . . And you know that after the
darkness, there will always be light.

So move through the tunnel towards the
light . . . Your shadow side may be accustomed
to the dark . . . and your guide may shed some
light on your path . . . Use them to help you
through the darkness . . . And don't forget . . .
that we all grow and experience new things . . .
and we learn . . . and we overcome . . . So
move through the tunnel . . . towards love and
light . . . As you move towards the light, you'll
feel it . . . and sense it . . . and the love . . . and
the energy.

When you come out of the tunnel. . . you'll see
all of the people in your life . . . sitting in an
open, outdoor amphitheater in front of you . . .
And the stage is yours . . . There are costumes
behind the stage that you may use . . . or you
may want to be yourself.

But the stage is there for you to dance . . . to
sing . . . to speak . . . to let the world . . . know
what you have to say to it.

You can feel the acceptance . . . You may hear
applause . . . Perhaps tears or laughter, when
appropriate . . . The people are with you . . .
They are loving you . . . They are enjoying
you . . . for what and who you are.

Yet you know inside you . . . that you don't
require applause to know when you have
performed well . . . when you have given . . .
all that is inside of you . . . When you have
participated . . . you are a winner.

That's something that's inside of you . . . that
you don't need someone else to tell you about.

When you complete your performance . . . take
some time . . . to go down into the audience . . .
to see how they receive you . . . and what they
would like to share with you . . . and you with
them . . . Take a moment now, to finish your
performance . . . and to share with your
audience.

When you are done . . . follow my voice . . .
and let it go with you . . . as you, your guide
and your shadow . . . find a quiet place along the
path to discuss what has happened.

You may want to present them with new
questions . . . new conflicts . . . new
problems . . . that have entered your life and
that you would like help in resolving . . . so
you'll free more energy for love and joy.

Sit down now with your guide and shadow to
discuss whatever you feel needs to be
shared . . . And take this time . . . They are here
for you.

When you are done . . . you may say goodbye to your shadow and guide and follow my voice again . . . But know that they are always available to you . . . in times of distress . . . to guide you . . . and to help you through the darkness . . . by bringing you light or helping you work in the dark.

Now continue on your path . . . Realize how strong you are . . . as you move along your path, on your own . . . And take a moment to enjoy, and accept your potential . . . You have gotten this far . . . You have survived . . . You have made it . . . And with more joy, and love, and hope in your life . . . it will become easier . . . and not harder.

The path . . . will unfold in front of you . . . And know that these lessons that you learn become a part of you . . . Know that your feelings are yours . . . You may choose joy . . . You may choose hope . . . You may choose love . . . You may choose to celebrate your life . . . No one creates your feelings . . . You do.

Know that whatever question appears . . . love is the answer . . . Love heals lives . . . Know that.

If you could love enough . . . you would be the most powerful . . . individual . . . that you have ever met . . . There is nothing that enough love can not conquer . . . There is nothing that enough love cannot heal.

To reach out . . . and to work . . . at becoming love . . . creates a very unique and special person . . . Accept and love yourself . . . for what you are attempting . . . And take a moment to truly look at yourself.

Pause for 10 seconds

What you have chosen . . . very few people choose . . . You are taking the time . . . to love . . . and accept . . . and nurture . . . to become a beautiful human being . . . You are taking the time to change the world . . . by changing yourself . . . You are what life is about . . . Life is to be experienced.

Pause for 10 seconds

When you are ready to follow my voice . . . come back . . . come back with the knowledge . . . The knowledge that very few people are willing to accept, but a knowledge that we all know deep down inside . . . And so let go.

Remember you were born totally lovable . . . If there is anything in your life that has made you question that love, it came from outside of you . . . And let go . . . let go of those messages . . . and accept yourself . . . and love yourself . . . and become one with yourself.

And let that self . . . become aware of your breathing . . . of the room . . . of the music . . . and slowly return filled with love . . . joy . . . hope . . . and optimism.

When you feel ready, open your "I" . . . and begin your journey.

Healing Yourself and the Universe

Patricia A. McPartland

Time: 20 minutes

In this script, participants relax and feel protected as past hurts and negativity are released and forgiven through the experience of being surrounded by a healing, loving light.

This meditation was developed as a result of the inspiring words of Father Rizzo, a noted healer. He believes that in order to heal, you must first wish well to yourself, wish well to others, and wish well to the universe. If you want to heal yourself, you must wish everyone and everything well. "You will not exclude but will include if you want to be a healer," says Father Rizzo. With these words in mind, take the participants on the following journey. Afterwards, have them talk about their experiences.

Script

It is time to stop talking and to be still a minute . . . Let your mind become clear of all thoughts. If your mind begins to wander, bring your attention back to the sound of my voice.

Feel yourself becoming more and more centered.

Take in a deep breath . . . and exhale slowly and completely.

Picture a bright, white light surrounding you . . . protecting you. This protective white light will ensure that only that which is good will come to you and only that which is good will come from you.

On your next in-breath, visualize our planet . . . Picture the globe suspended in space . . . Become aware of the continents and the blue ocean waters. See the earth spinning in space . . . Visualize a world that is full of peace . . . joy . . . and love.

The flowers, plants, and herbs grow in abundance and all the people of the world are nourished from the planet's fruits . . . Plenty of food and clean water is available for all of us. We share the fruits of the earth with each other and give freely. We honor the animals and the environment and all the inhabitants in it.

As you experience honor for all the earth's inhabitants, visualize those who have harmed or hurt you in some way and send these individuals love, understanding, and healing light.

Spend some time now forgiving each and every person who has given you pain, and send a healing, loving thought to each one of them.

Feel or see a powerful, cleansing, healing light surrounding your mother ... your father ... your sisters ... your brothers ... your friends ... your children ... your former husbands or wives or lovers ... your present husband or wife or lover ... your in-laws ... uncles and aunts ... nieces and nephews ... cousins ... politicians ... teachers.

See a powerful, cleansing light surrounding everyone who may have harmed you. Recall some of these people and surround them with a loving, healing light.

Pause

Now send a loving, healing light to all those who have helped you. Visualize each and every one of these people.

Long pause

Visualize your pets ... the dogs, cats, horses, birds, and farm animals that bring so much love and joy into your lives. Send all these animals health and love.

It is now time to send a loving, healing light to yourself, forgiving yourself for all your indiscretions, forgiving yourself for your mistakes.

Now let the good things you have done come to
mind . . . Give yourself the honor you
deserve . . . Send loving, healing light to
yourself, for you are well, whole, and balanced
in mind, body, and spirit.

Now it is time to slowly bring this healing
journey to an end. Know that you can always
heal yourself, your relationships, and all that is a
part of the universe.

As you come back to the present, you feel a
strong sense of inner contentment, joy, personal
strength, and good feelings . . . as you return to
the present moment.

Begin to stretch whenever you are ready and
open your eyes.

Repeat the above instructions until everyone is alert.

Sun Meditation for Healing

Judy Fulop and Julie T. Lusk

Time: 10 minutes

In this script, participants experience the healing power and energy of the sun as they imagine it warming and relaxing them.

Script

Allow yourself to become as relaxed and comfortable as you can . . . Let your body feel supported by the ground underneath you.

Slowly begin to see or feel yourself lying in a grassy meadow with the sun shining it's golden rays gently upon you . . . Let yourself soak in these warm rays . . . taking in the healing power and life giving energy of the sunshine.

This magnificent ball of light has been a sustaining source of energy for millions of years and will be an energy source for millions of years to come . . . The ancient sun is the same sun which shined down upon the dinosaurs . . . upon the Egyptians while they built the pyramids . . . and it shines upon the earth and all the other planets in our solar system and will continue to do so forever.

As the sun's rays gently touch your skin, allow
the warmth and energy to flow slowly through
your body . . . pulsing through your bones . . .
sending healing light to your organs . . .
flowing to your tissues . . . recharging every
system . . . and now settling into your
innermost being . . . your heart center.

Sense your heart center glowing with this
radiant energy, if you wish, give it a color . . .
Take a few moments to allow this warm and
healing energy to reach your innermost
being . . . physically . . . emotionally . . .
mentally . . . and spiritually.

Pause for 30 seconds

As this healing energy grows and expands,
allow yourself to see, feel, and sense this energy
surrounding your being . . . growing and
growing . . . Allow this energy to expand
further and fill this room . . . this building . . .
surrounding this town . . . spreading
throughout our state . . . to our country . . . and
out into the world . . . and finally throughout
the universe . . . reaching and touching and
blessing all.

Pause for 30 seconds

You may share this healing energy and power
with anyone you are aware of right now . . .
Mentally ask them if they are willing to receive

this healing energy ... If they are ... send this source of healing energy to them ... giving them the time they need to take in this energy and make it theirs in their own heart center.

If they are not willing or ready for this energy right now, put this energy within their reach and invite them to reach out for this energy when they need it.

Pause for 30 seconds

Now take your attention back to your own heart center ... Find a safe place within you to keep this healing and powerful energy ... a place to keep it protected and within your reach ... Give yourself permission to get in touch with this energy whenever you wish.

With the warmth of this energy in your being, begin stretching, wiggling, and moving ... Slowly open your eyes, feeling alive, refreshed, keenly alert, and completely healthy.

Repeat the above instructions until everyone is alert.

Vitamin T Imagery

Bob Czimbal

Time: 25 minutes

In this script, participants absorb Vitamin T, the nurturing nutrient found in healthy touch, by imagining they are receiving a massage.

You may help participants explore their memories of being touched by asking what kind of touch they received as infants, young children, teenagers, and adults. Who were the people in their lives who gave out regular doses of Vitamin T?

Script

Relax by using your mind to touch different parts of your body in a healthy way.

Please close your eyes and gently breathe in . . . and out . . . in . . . and out . . . in . . . and out.

You are going to be using your mind to give yourself a body massage. Bring to mind someone that you trust completely to give you an expert body massage. This may be someone you know already or someone new.

Imagine that you are lying on your stomach.

Allow your mind to focus on your feet . . .
imagine you're having your feet massaged with
lotion that is deeply, slowly relaxing all the
muscles in your feet . . . The lotion smells so
good.

Now imagine that lotion is being rubbed into
your ankles and calves . . . into and around
your knees. You are getting generous amounts
of Vitamin Touch . . . Feel health pouring over
you.

With each breath in and out, feel the massaging
of the muscles in your lower legs, kneading
deeply into the muscles, releasing the
tension . . . As you breathe in and as you
breathe out, allow yourself to let go . . . Let go
more and more as you are rubbed.

Now feel your mind focusing on your thighs,
feeling again as if a massage therapist were
gently rubbing your thighs with lotion . . . up
and down . . . up and down . . . helping these
large muscles to let go and relax.

Now feel yourself receiving healthy touch to
your hips. Feel the lotion gently working on
your hips, deep into the muscles, very deep . . .
feel yourself letting go, each time you exhale . . .
Allow yourself to fully enjoy the experience of
receiving Vitamin T.

Your personal massage therapist is now

applying lotion to your back muscles, working up and down your spine . . . right and left . . . working these muscles that support you, that hold you, that take care of you.

And now give your muscles permission to let go and to relax completely. Feel your therapist's fingers working deep into the muscles.

Now go on to the muscles of your neck. Feel how you can let go, no longer needing to support your head . . . Feeling the fingertips working deep into the muscles . . . As you breathe in, and out, you let go and relax. Breathe in . . . and out . . . Practice absorbing relaxation as you inhale. Breathe in . . . And as you exhale, let go of the tension.

Now you are gently rolled onto your back, and your massage continues on your stomach and torso, massaging all the muscles in and around your abdomen and working up across your chest and up to your shoulders.

Breathe in . . . and out, letting go of tension as you exhale . . . Allow this mental massage to help you absorb megadoses of Vitamin T. Remember that you deserve healthy touch.

Feel the massage proceeding down your arms, to your elbows, down to your wrists, and into your hands and fingers . . . Notice how deeply your body has relaxed as you imagine receiving a wonderful massage. You are totally relaxed from the neck on down.

Now focus all your attention on your face, your scalp. Feel how your massage therapist is gently working through all the muscles in your face, especially your jaw muscles . . . and around the eyes.

Breathe in . . . breathe out, and relax as you let go . . . Feel your massage being finished by a very soft and gentle massage to your scalp, and all around your ears . . . Let go of the last remaining bit of tension.

Let Vitamin T heal all of your ouches. Let Vitamin T restore you to balance and health and happiness . . . Allow your body to deeply relax, deeper than you've ever relaxed before. And as you relax deeper and deeper, you feel lighter and lighter.

Pause for 10 seconds

Now feel that a very strong person is coming to pick you up, coming to hold you, coming to rock you . . . Allow yourself to be rocked and cradled and held as if you were as light as a baby . . . back and forth . . . back and forth, enjoying the contact, enjoying the motion, allowing yourself to absorb all of the Vitamin T that you can.

Pause

Bring your attention back to your breath. Now with all your attention focused on your breath, take in a long, deep breath . . . and now let your breath out.

Take in another long, deep breath . . . and then let all the air out . . . With each breath you begin to feel alert and refreshed.

Let your breath return to normal . . . Stretch out when you are ready . . . And when you open up your eyes, you will feel alert and refreshed.

Repeat the above instructions until everyone is alert.

Food for Thought: Imagery for Weight Control

Constance Kirk

Time: 15 minutes

In this script, participants learn to think differently about food, about dieting, and about themselves by stimulating their ability to make informed choices. This script is designed to take the struggle out of weight loss and weight maintenance while increasing the joy that should accompany positive changes.

Participants should practice these imagery techniques at least twice per day until making good choices becomes easier and their perceptions of food change.

Note: You may want to use a relaxation exercise prior to this visualization.

Script

Sit back and relax. Surrender to the messages and images. Symbolic imagery works just as well, and sometimes better, than concrete representations of the "real thing." Your body has its own wisdom . . . The images and language used here are no more than suggestions that ask or direct the body in very general ways to do the things you want it to do.

When you give the body *positive* messages, trust your body's wisdom to manifest the results. The body knows what to do and how to do it. In fact, too much intellectualization just gets in the way.

Know that giving yourself this opportunity to rest and learn is a gift to yourself; you deserve this gift.

Imagine how you will look and feel when you reach your ideal weight and body composition ... How will you look?

Pause for 10 seconds

Imagine youself as you are right now looking in a steam-covered mirror. As you begin to wipe the steam off, the new you, your ideal self, is reflected ... How do you feel?

The person in the mirror smiles and reflects happiness and joy. How do you move? ... Feel the freedom of movement.

Soak in the essence of this feeling ... When you are feeling exhilarated and confident, clench your fists and say to yourself, "YES."

Pause for 1 minute

From now on, every time you eat take a moment to create the image you have here and anchor the confident feeling it gives you by

127

clenching your fist and saying a resounding
YES!

Notice how powerful you feel right now . . .
This positive image *you* created produced this
powerful state. Any time during the day or
night when you feel low, weak, or depressed,
bring this image back . . . You will then create
your own power right when you need it.

We can even make the process easier by
changing the perception we have of food. When
we truly know food beyond the level of taste
and smell, perception changes.

One of the surest and fastest ways to lose weight
is to decrease the amount of dietary fat you eat.
This seems difficult for many people because
they like the taste of fat; fat does give a great
deal of flavor to foods . . . If you think about it,
though, it is rather dangerous if not downright
stupid to base decisions on one sense—taste—
one tiny bit of information which stimulates a
modicum of pleasure.

Living your life in a healthy vibrant body is
much more pleasurable. So let's see and
experience dietary fat beyond taste.

Imagine a very large man eating and enjoying
high-fat foods . . . a T-bone steak, rolls with
butter, a baked potato with lots of butter and

sour cream, an ice cream sundae. You may even find yourself getting hungry or salivating.

This meal is providing the man with many more calories than he needs, with about 75 percent of the calories coming from fat. The fat calories outweigh his real needs.

Imagine the following as vividly as you can.

See the fat he has eaten entering and expanding the size of his fat cells . . . No wonder he is overweight . . .The fat enters his blood stream from the intestines and makes the elements of his blood sticky, very sticky . . . See the fat clumping together in his bloodstream . . . It is getting so thick that it cannot get through the capillaries. A traffic jam results with little oxygen and carbon dioxide removal in 30 percent of the tissues . . . He gets drowsy and sluggish.

Cholesterol is deposited in the lining of the blood vessels making them hard and inflexible . . . The deposits look like stalactites and stalagmites in a cave . . . High blood pressure, heart disease, and the risk of having a stroke increase . . . Fat slows down the rate of speed that food passes through the intestines. It lingers in the intestine, and as it breaks down it produces carcinogenic substances that increase the probability of cancer.

Every time you see high-fat foods, imagine the harm these foods can do . . . *Never* imagine harmful things happening in your own body!

Focus on what you can have instead of what you cannot have. Imagine the reverse of what you just saw. See yourself in a restaurant looking at the menu and seeing only the good and nourishing food choices.

As you imagine yourself eating, see the gift you are giving your body—blood flowing smoothly in clean arteries . . . fat cells staying the same size or decreasing in size . . . energy stabilizing . . . and the heart functioning more properly.

Every time you make the best choice you have given yourself a gift of health and energy. You can and do savor good, nourishing food.

Now shifting your attention . . . choose a situation in which you found yourself in the past having a difficult time controlling your eating. Sometimes this is a painful thing to remember.

Pause for 15 seconds

Imagine the situation as though you are an observer . . . detached, watching from afar . . . Even though it is uncomfortable, you need not fear it, because it is in the past. Let the details of the situation become clear.

Pause for 15 seconds

Now quickly shift your attention to the image of yourself looking in the mirror at your ideal self and size . . . See it . . . Feel it . . . Clench your fist and say, "YES!" When you feel powerful, step into the old scene with a sense of power and control.

Pause for 10 seconds

Remember, in your imagination you can do ANYTHING!

For a moment, practice seeing . . . hearing . . . and feeling your powerful self acting in the way you truly wish to act . . . acting in the way that will get you the results you want.

Pause for 15 seconds

Imagine your self-confidence growing and becoming stronger. It is easy and natural . . . There is enjoyment and freedom in making these life-affirming decisions . . . Notice the people around you reinforcing and acknowledging you in supportive ways.

Every time you practice this mental rehearsal, you increase the probability of truly acting that way when the situation arises again.

Slowly let the images go and focus your attention on your breathing.

Pause for 10 seconds

Remember that you now have the skill and resourcefulness to control your eating habits any time you need to. You accept your challenge as an opportunity to grow. You will know when your perception is changed, when making poor food choices is more difficult and uncomfortable than making good food choices. What a switch!

Practice . . . practice . . . practice. Remember, you can practice imagery anywhere. Good luck.

Begin to stretch . . . feeling relaxed, refreshed, and confident . . . Open your eyes slowly and feel a sense of renewed commitment and power.

Repeat the above instructions until everyone is alert.

Breastfeeding

Judy Schwakopf

Time: 20 minutes

In this guided meditation, mothers visualize the miraculous nursing process while nursing their babies.

Script

Turn on music that helps you relax . . . Prepare yourself by clearing your mind of all "what if's" . . . "need to's" . . . "want to's" . . . and "should do's" . . . Remove any distractions that can interfere with this special time.

Place a "Do Not Disturb" sign on your door . . . disconnect the phone . . . turn the television off . . . empty your bladder . . . remove pets to another room, unless they enhance your relaxation . . . Change your baby's diaper or soiled clothing.

Make something to drink—ice water, fruit juice, milk , decaffeinated tea, whatever you like . . . Place it in a location convenient to your nursing "niche."

Find your own most comfortable and

comforting haven for nursing—a rocking chair, recliner, bed, or sofa. Choose whatever will help you relax most easily . . . Position yourself and your baby with pillows . . . Take your time, nestle in . . . Settle in with your baby, skin to skin.

Put other concerns . . . meals to prepare . . . phone calls to return . . . physical or mental fatigue . . . in mental boxes . . . to be opened when your baby has finished nursing and is contentedly resting . . . Concentrate on the here and now . . . and your desire to nurse your baby.

Savor the softness . . . take in the sweet baby smell . . . The center of the universe has shifted . . . it is here . . . it is now . . . nurturing . . . nourishing this new young love of your life.

Take in a deep, cleansing breath . . . Release your tensions as you let your breath out . . . Gently place your baby to your breast . . . Stroke your baby's lips with your nipple and help your baby take in as much of the darker areola as possible.

As you nourished and protected your unborn child, so will you continue to nourish and protect the infant nursing at your breast.

Your body was made for this special time . . .
The chemistry within you . . . the hormones
surging to produce and deliver sweet mother's
milk for your baby . . . all are part of a wonderful process that connects you, once again, to this
life you created and carried within you.

The sucking . . . fierce and searching . . . or
calm and steady . . . stimulates nerve endings in
your nipples which signal your body to release
oxytocin.

Baby's tongue under the nipple . . . baby's jaw
compressing the areola . . . sending
messages . . . unspoken . . . Look at your
baby . . . asking so little . . . receiving so much.

A wondrous stream of milk is released as the
oxytocin travels through your blood stream to
the breast . . . See the alveolus glands creating
the milk from vitamins and minerals and
nutrients you take in for yourself and your baby.

See the leafy green and bright yellow vegetables,
the breads, the milk and cheese, the fruits and
juices, meat, fish, eggs, and beans you eat.

Sense the nutrients entering your bloodstream,
making their way to the alveolus glands to make
good milk for your baby.

Think of the good foods you eat and the extra

fluids you drink for your good health and for your baby . . . The sleep and rest you need . . . and take when you can . . . helps make more good milk for your baby.

Feel the tugging at your breast as your baby sends messages with oxytocin, making your muscles contract around your alveolus glands . . . Sense the tingling sensation of "let down" as your milk is squeezed from your alveolus glands . . . through sturdy ductules . . . into milk pods under your areola.

See the pools filling with milk . . . replenished easily by the productive alveolus glands . . . Each compression of your baby's jaw releases milk from the filled pools . . . The milk, marvelously created . . . eagerly awaited . . . flows through the nipple to your baby.

You may feel tingling and the release of milk from your other breast . . . full and ready for your baby to nurse.

Watch your baby suckle, swallow, and rest . . . Breathe slowly . . . deeply . . . evenly . . . Feel this gift of milk and love leaving your body and entering your baby's . . . Enjoy the closeness and the chance to slow down for this small part of your day.

While you are giving ... let yourself
receive ... tenderness ... peace ... calm ...
contentment ... a unique closeness ... in this
gift of nursing.

Using imagery to encourage self-esteem, offer positive affirmations, focus on personal growth and development, and increase people's ability to imagine sights, sounds, and other physical sensations are the main goals of these guided meditations.

a painter's life. For example, Picasso had his Blue Period, Pink Period, Cubist Period, and a dozen other periods throughout his life. Your life passes through phases as well.   (20 minutes)

You Are a Child Again   156

In this script, participants imagine they are children again. Children who have fun playing and moving, are confident and self-assured, and unconditionally loved.   (5 minutes)

Flower Meditation   159

In this visualization script, participants increase their ability to imagine seeing, touching, smelling, and feeling.   (20 minutes)

A Meditation of a World Vision   163

In this guided meditation, participants experience their connection to the life-force of the universe by lying on the ground and imagining the earth's energy coming through them.   (15 minutes)

Addiction to Wellness

Donald B. Ardell

Time: 10 minutes

In this script, participants seek physical, mental, psychological, and spiritual wellness. Positive self-esteem is nurtured.

Script

Now create a mental image of the best possible PHYSICAL you ... How do you appear ... Have fun and imagine what you can do with your ideal body ... See how it feels to spread your arms ... to stretch your legs ... and to flex those muscles honed for speed, endurance, and power.

It feels great ... Enjoy it ... Take another deep breath to fill those high-powered lungs and watch yourself with your mind's eye take that splendid body for a few leaps in the air ... Let it get better, even more fun.

Now see yourself running in a road race, bounding past each mile marker, well ahead of any pace you thought within your capability. Note that you are feeling STRONGER as you go along ... Notice the power, the grace and the speed that is yours as you triumphantly near the crowd at the finish line. Hear the crowd cheering you.

Breathe deeply once more and give thanks for this spectacular physical gift that is in your control. It is a wonderful feeling.

It is true that in addition to good fortune, good genes, and a favorable environment, you owe so much of your success with this body to the fact that you have CHOSEN wellness. Having made that choice, you now support it each day with a lifestyle of excellence. Physically you crave this sensation of excellence. You are positively addicted to it.

Envision the experience of PSYCHOLOGICAL excellence . . . Reflect on the advantages of being the kind of person you are, beyond the physical magnificence of your being, and acknowledge yourself emotionally mature and whole.

Breathe deeply and give yourself a well deserved mental bow . . . Indulge in another of those deep breaths.

In the privacy of your thoughts, cover yourself with glorious compliments . . . Nurture your self-esteem in positive and healthy ways . . . What a glorious specimen of emotional and physiological well-being you are. You have fashioned, over the course of many years, a record of lifestyle artistry.

Shift now to images of the ideal MENTAL state that you enjoy . . . Take note of even a partial list of your MENTAL strengths.

You think clearly . . . you solve problems effortlessly and creatively, and are full of wonderful, new ideas . . . You have a great sense of humor . . . You are committed to many standards of personal excellence . . . You are disciplined to exercise vigorously and can't imagine engaging in destructive habits. You actually PREFER to eat sensibly. You are connected to people who love you whom you care about very deeply . . . You enjoy your work, and your avocational interests, and your future looks bright.

Finally, fashion a picture in your mind of SPIRITUAL excellence. Enjoy the EXPERIENCE of fulfillment with your purposes, beliefs, values, and sense of meaning.

Like so many people in our society, you are addicted, but not to worseness. You are dependent on daily doses of joy, purpose, meaning, and variety in your daily life.

You are dependent on yourself, even though

you know that you are connected with others . . . You are addicted to wellness.

Pause

Know that you are a unique being, unlike any creature to walk the earth in its 4.6 billion years of existence . . . and that there will never be another like you, not in another 4.6 billion years or any time thereafter.

Pause

Yes, you're pretty amazing as a wellness addict.

Why keep such a good thing all to yourself? Try becoming a wellness pusher. Continue to model the benefits of your splendid habits and attitudes for others in a helpful manner . . . and we will soon see many others enjoying wellness.

Now stretch and open your eyes, feeling refreshed and alert.

Repeat the above instruction until everyone is alert.

Body Image Visualization

Lauve Metcalfe

Time: 25 minutes

In this visualization script, participants picture their own body images and practice positive affirmations to promote self-esteem and inner beauty.

Script

Begin taking deep breaths. With every inhalation, fill your body with positive energy . . . With every exhalation, feel all of the negative energy being released from your body.

Continue to breathe deeply, focusing on bringing in the positive energy as you breathe in, and letting go of the negative energy as your breath is released.

Now focus your attention on your body, all the different parts of your body . . . You will begin to do a "body check" that will bring you in touch with your physical body and create an awareness of your body parts.

First focus on your feet and legs . . . Breathe in positive energy to your feet and legs, and breathe out negative thoughts and energy.

Now focus on your thighs and hips . . . breathe in positive energy to your thighs and hips, and breathe out negative thoughts and energy.

Move up your body and focus on your buttocks and abdomen. Breathe in positive energy to your buttocks and abdomen, and breathe out negative thoughts and energy.

Now bring your attention and focus to your back and shoulders, breathing in positive energy to your back and shoulders, and breathing out negative thoughts and energy.

Now bring your focus to your upper and lower arms and hands. Breathe in positive energy to your upper and lower arms and hands . . . and breathe out negative thoughts and energy.

Focus on your neck, head, and hair. Breathe in positive energy to your neck, head, and hair . . . Breathe out negative thoughts and feelings.

Focus on your face, and particularly your eyes, nose, and mouth . . . Breathe in positive energy to these areas and breathe out negative thoughts and feelings.

How do your feel about your feet, calves, and upper legs? . . . Do they feel heavy and sluggish? ... tense? ... or maybe light and relaxed? ... Get in touch with the feelings you have towards your feet, calves, and upper legs.

Move your concentration up to your hips and buttocks, and again, get in touch with the feelings you have for your buttocks and hips. Do they feel heavy and fat? ... perhaps strong and smooth?

Draw your attention on up to your abdominal area ... then to your chest ... and upper back ... Now to your shoulders, arms, neck, and head ... How do these areas of your body feel to you?

Once you have taken enough time to do a body check and have thought about how you are feeling, begin again. But this time repeat silently after me a positive affirmation for each body part and for each area of your body. If your mind begins to wander, or if you deny or doubt the affirmation, acknowledge your discomfort to yourself and then bring your attention back to the affirmation and repeat it silently and as confidently as you can.

As you continue to practice positive self-talk through affirmations, you will begin to see a shift in your mindset and begin to create positive, healthy body affirmations that become a regular part of your psyche.

My feet are a wonderful support for my body . . . I take care of them and respond to their needs.

Repeat this affirmation silently to yourself to give participants time to say the affirmation silently to themselves. Repeat this for each affirmation.

My calves, knees, and thighs are strong and beautiful and give me sound support for the rest of my body . . . They are just right the way they are . . . My legs take me where I want to go . . . I move with coordination, grace and ease . . . My legs are just right for who I am.

My hips and buttocks are smooth and strong . . . I take care of them and respond to their needs . . . I take care of my hips and buttocks by exercising and eating well . . . My hips and buttocks are just right for me right now.

My back is healthy, strong yet flexible . . . My spine gives me all the support I need, and it feels good, strong, and healthy.

My stomach and chest are just right for who I am . . . My stomach and chest are a positive expression of my health and well-being . . . My digestive system digests my food and nourishes my body . . . My heart is strong and beats in perfect rhythm.

147

My shoulders, arms, and hands suit my needs just the way they are ... My arms are strong ... My hands express my talents to their fullest ... They allow me to touch others in my special and unique way ... They allow me to be touched by others in a positive way.

My neck supports my head and my head is perfectly balanced upon my neck and shoulders ... My hair is healthy and strong ... My eyes see clearly and sparkle with my inner beauty ... My nose allows me to breathe deeply and energizes my body with each breath ... My ears hear clearly and allow me to appreciate the sounds of life ... My mind is sharp and my thoughts are positive.

My attitudes and perceptions about myself are positive ... I honor my body and make choices that are healthy and respectful of myself ... Every day in every way, I am better and better ... I continue to create a health centered approach to living that nurtures every part of me.

Continue to bathe yourself with positive affirmations, personalizing each thought to your own needs.

Pause for 1 minute

Now bring your attention back to your whole body ... Let your attention sweep up from

your feet and legs to your torso and shoulders
and down your arms, over to your hips and up
your back to your neck, head, and face.
Breathe fully and deeply once again. On the
inhalation, bring positive energies into your
body. On the exhalation, feel the positive
energies spreading throughout your entire
being.

Let your breath return to normal. Silently count
from 5 to 1, stretch and then open your eyes.
5 ... 4 ... 3 ... 2 ... 1 ... Stretch and then
open your eyes.

Repeat the above instructions until everyone is alert.

OM Visitation

Judd Allen

Time: Unlimited

In this script, participants meditate on the word "OM" to help them connect with people they love, but who are far away.

Chanting OM is a universal meditation that can bring people into community with their surroundings and with the world. OM can either be pronounced like Home, dropping the H, or it can be pronounced ooooooooooo aaaaaaaahhhhhhhhhhhmmmm.

This meditation is best practiced when alone and in a quiet place, free from outside noise and distractions.

Script

Sit on the floor with your legs crossed and your eyes closed. Rest your arms comfortably on your lap and touch your thumb and first finger together.

Begin by breathing fully and deeply, filling your lungs to capacity, letting the breath go all the way in and all the way out until you quiet your mind and fill yourself with life sustaining air.

Say the word OM out loud as you breathe out, feeling the vibrations of the sounds beginning in your belly . . . flowing up through your throat . . . and then to the top of your head . . . and out into the world.

As you breathe in, say OM silently to yourself. Continue to repeat your OM chant forcefully and fully, taking your time to release your breath completely while also saying OM. Repeat this until you are completely focused on the full and powerful sound of your voice.

Think of someone that you love or would like to feel a connection with. Experience how your OM is traveling to the person you have in mind. Visualize this person being surrounded and embraced by the vibrations of your voice. Repeat chanting OM until you feel a sense of unity and connection with that person.

If you wish, repeat the process while thinking of someone else.

Pause

When you have finished your visitations, stop saying OM and concentrate on your breathing. Bring your mind back into your immediate surroundings. When ready, open your eyes, feeling a strong sense of inner joy and connection to others.

Repeat the above instructions until everyone is alert.

The Blue Period

Tom Ferguson

Time: 20 minutes

In this empowerment script, participants observe their lives to discover trends and patterns that are occurring. This script parallels the way an art historian might look at a painter's life. For example, Picasso had his Blue Period, Pink Period, Cubist Period, and a dozen other periods throughout his life. Your life passes through phases as well.

Script

Close your eyes . . . allow yourself to begin settling down . . . Sit in silence for a moment.

Now bring your attention to your breath . . . As you breathe out, imagine that any stress in your body is passing out with the exhaled air . . . Just feel the stress passing out of your body and drifting far . . . far away . . . leaving you refreshed . . . happy . . . and very relaxed.

Let yourself be as comfortable as you're willing to allow yourself to be . . . There's no place you need to go right now . . . Nothing that you need to do . . . No problems that you need to solve . . . Let yourself begin feeling centered.

Just let yourself relax . . . Let yourself relax more and more . . . As your eyelids grow heavier and heavier . . . your breathing becomes deeper . . . slower . . . and more regular. Allow all the immediate worries and preoccupations of the day to slip away.

Now let your mind drift back over the recent months and years . . . and ask yourself, where am I in my life right now?

Imagine that you are looking at your life in the way an art historian might look at a painter's life . . . Picasso had his Blue Period . . . his Pink Period . . . his Cubist period . . . and a dozen other periods . . . So what have been the major periods of your own life?

Pause for 10 seconds

What would your *present* period be? . . . What are the characteristics of this period of your life? . . . What name would you give to this period? . . . What is the period of your life in which you find yourself right now?

Pause for 10 seconds

This period may have begun very recently, or it may extend back many years. It may have started with a new relationship . . . a new job . . . or a move of some sort.

153

Perhaps it began with an idea for a new project . . . maybe a marriage, or the birth of a child. Did it begin with an illness or injury . . . a loss . . . a separation . . . or a death? . . .

Is the current period of your life a time of hard work or a time of fallowness . . . of satisfaction or dissatisfaction . . . a time of ending or a time of beginning?

Perhaps it began with an easily identifiable event, or it may be a period characterized by a general quality of feeling . . . a pervasive enthusiasm or a cloud of depression . . . Perhaps this is a time of renewal . . . Or is it a time of mid-life or other changes?

Let your mind wander . . . Don't attempt to direct your thinking . . . Let your mind go . . . Simply sit in silence and allow the thoughts and feelings to come . . . to allow the movement of this most recent period of your life to emerge, without analyzing or judging . . . Just let it be . . . Simply allow yourself to be in a condition of openness, of readiness, and allow the boundaries and characteristics of this present period of your life to take shape.

You may find that spontaneous answers to these questions begin to suggest themselves.

What is this present period of my life?

How far back does it go?

What events mark it off?

What have been the main characteristics of this period?

What can I call this period of my life?

What is the path I now need to travel?

What is it now that I most need to empower myself to do?

Pause for 30 seconds

And now gradually return your attention to your breathing . . . Feel the air passing out and passing in . . . Feel your fingers . . . and your toes as you gradually, slowly begin to wiggle and stretch them . . . Stretch your shoulders and arms . . . Open your mouth and stretch your jaw muscles . . . stretch your neck, from side to side . . . And when you're ready, gradually, slowly open your eyes.

Repeat the above instructions until everyone is alert.

This script has been adapted from an article that Tom Ferguson wrote with Ira Progoff for *Medical Self-Care* magazine several years ago. Progoff is the author of *At a Journal Workshop*, a wonderful guide to keeping a psychological journal.

You Are a Child Again

Barbara Kyle

Time: 5 minutes

In this script, participants imagine they are children again. Children who have fun playing and moving, are confident and self-assured, and unconditionally loved.

Note: You may want to use a relaxation exercise prior to this visualization.

Script

Together, let us step into the stillness of this moment with a relaxed body and a peaceful mind . . . You are in perfect peace.

Open your mind and expand your imagination . . . Come with me . . . See what I see . . . Hear what I hear . . . You are a child again. Yes, a child . . . Beautiful, loving, and free . . . Just as you were created . . . You are so beautiful, so very wonderful . . . Your face has a radiant glow . . . Your eyes sparkle with an inner light . . . Your dazzling smile is a pure delight . . . You are a child again.

I see you moving with a perfect grace and flow as if the world was made just for you . . . You

are a child again ... I see you running
effortlessly with outstretched arms, eager to
meet your good surroundings ... You chase a
beautiful butterfly in flight and laugh joyfully as
it eludes you and flutters out of sight ... You
are a child again.

You feel like moving ... You need to run and
play ... Your boundless energy is forever and
a day ... You are happy ... Each day you
celebrate, as I see you swirling and twirling in a
circle free with your arms above your head.
Caught up in time splendidly. Free ... yes ...
free to love ... to do ... to be. You are a child
again.

All your needs are satisfied from the rich
outpouring of a loving father and mother. All
things are possible because you are loved ...
You give thanks ... You believe ... You trust.

Come dance for me ... Sing your sweet little
song ... Love with your rare, unconditional
love ... Open up your heart. You are a child
again.

If by chance you sometimes forget and say, "I
am so small, I'm just a little one." The answer
will come: "I am your strength. You are strong
enough" ... Feel your strength.

If you have doubts and think, *I make mistakes.*

There is so much I do not know. The answer will come: "I am your knowledge. You are wise enough" . . . Feel your wisdom now.

If you sometimes feel, *I am afraid, I lose my courage and I run away.* The answer will come. "Take heart my child. It is all an illusion. I am but a breath away. You are protected. . . . You are a beloved child . . . A child of the universe . . . whole, and free, and perfect."

Pause

Feel yourself returning to your own wonderful body . . . your own age . . . feeling a sense of completeness and ready for anything.

Start to wiggle and stretch, and when you are ready, open your eyes with the feeling of being refreshed and alert.

Repeat the above instructions until everyone is alert.

Flower Meditation

Julie T. Lusk

Time: 20 minutes

In this visualization script, participants increase their ability to imagine seeing, touching, smelling, and feeling.

Note: Obtain fresh flowers for participants before using this script.

Script

Visualization

Place the flowers at eye level in front of you . . . Gently gaze at them without straining your eyes . . . Look softly at the shapes of the flowers, stems, and leaves . . . Become aware of their shapes and sizes. See their colors.

After you have spent a few minutes looking carefully at the flowers, close your eyes and visualize the flowers in your imagination. When the visualization becomes difficult, open up your eyes and look at the flowers once again. Close your eyes once more and recreate a vision of the flowers. Repetition will increase your ability to visualize images in the mind's eye.

Touching and Feeling

Reach out and touch the flowers, stems, and leaves. Take your time to discover how the flowers feel . . . Explore the softness of the flowers and the feel of the stems and leaves. Discover their moistness.

Investigate the physical sensations of touching the bouquet of flowers. Run your fingers through the bouquet and listen to the sound of touching them . . . Allow the sense of touch to sink in through your fingertips and into your memory.

Stop touching the flowers and close your eyes. Experience the sense of touch through your memory . . . When the memory of touch begins to fade, reach out and touch the flowers with your fingers. And then imagine touching the flowers once again.

Smell

Bury your nose and take a full, deep breath. Let the flowers tickle your nose. Smell the fragrance and the freshness of the flowers. Enjoy.

Remember how the flowers smell and recreate the aroma in your imagination. Keep practicing until you are able to imagine the scent of the flowers from memory.

Thoughts and Feelings

Sit quietly and reflect upon the magnificence of the flowers. Open yourself up for new insights and realizations.

Integration

Relax, close your eyes, and imagine looking at a glorious bouquet of flowers . . . You may imagine any kind of flower you wish . . . roses . . . daisies . . . mums . . . baby's breath . . . marigolds . . . bird of paradise . . . any type of flowers you wish.

See the radiant colors . . . the rich reds . . . luscious yellows . . . deep purples . . . pure whites . . . soft pinks . . . gorgeous oranges . . . all the shades of green.

Become aware of the textures . . . patterns . . . and shapes of the petals . . . Look at the leaves . . . and the stems . . . Observe the flowers in their various degrees of unfoldment.

This time, imagine reaching out and touching the flowers . . . Feel the softness . . . their moistness . . . the texture of the petals . . . leaves . . . and stems . . . Imagine rubbing the flowers with your fingers . . . Touch the flowers . . . Feel them.

Experience touching the flowers . . . Run your fingers through the flowers and listen to what you hear.

Now imagine the scents and fragrances of the flowers . . . Breathe in their perfume . . . Smell the aroma . . . Fill up your lungs with the fresh smell of the flowers.

Take some time to think about the diversity and beauty of the flowers that grow for our enjoyment . . . Think about the life cycle of the flower . . . Enjoy.

Pause

When you are ready, open your eyes and stretch.

Repeat the above instruction until everyone is alert.

A Meditation of a World Vision

Karen G. Lane

Time: 15 minutes

In this guided meditation, participants experience their connection to the life-force of the universe by lying on the ground and imagining the earth's energy coming through them.

Script

Lie down on the floor . . . Feel your body on the floor. Imagine you are lying down on the earth, on a grassy knoll, or on a warm, sandy beach . . . wherever you feel most comfortable lying on the ground . . . on the earth.

If you wish, imagine you are lying on a light blanket. Imagine one under you . . . Feel it right now . . . Feel your body lying on the ground . . . Feel the places where your body touches the earth.

As you become aware of these places, these points of contact, you will begin letting each part become heavy . . . so heavy . . . and you'll allow each part to release and be received by the strongest, steadiest, most comfortable and comforting arms you can imagine.

Take a deep breath and release all the tension.

Feel your feet . . . your heels . . . heavy against
the earth . . . your calves . . . knees . . .
released, supported . . . thighs, sinking into the
ground and released . . . buttocks . . . lower
back . . . your spine . . . easing toward the
ground.

All along your spine and up into your neck . . .
your shoulders . . . let them feel heavy . . .
released onto the loving support of the earth.

Let your upper arms go . . . elbows . . .
forearms . . . wrists . . . hands . . . They're all
heavy and supported . . . just to be
supported . . . easing down.

Take an audible deep breath

Allow your head to be supported . . . just to be
supported . . . Your whole body, your entire
being is being held and supported.

Take a deep breath and release all tensions . . .
all concerns . . . Let all concerns just fall
away . . . be assured that they'll still be there
when you get up . . . but for now, just be . . .
here . . . supported.

Let your breathing find its own rhythm . . .
in . . . and out . . . an easy flow . . . with your

shoulders and back released and relaxed on the earth ... your chest expands and moves freely ... effortlessly ... breathing in and out ... smoothly ... easily ... allowing refreshing air to just flow through your being ... all the way down to your toes ... all through your body.

Become aware of your heartbeat ... the steady, constant rhythm of your heart ... Feel the pulsing ... the flow of blood ... of energy ... through your body ... Feel the steady rhythm of your heart ... Feel it.

Now become aware of the earth beneath you once again ... Imagine that the earth's energy is flowing and pulsing ... steady and unending ... like a heartbeat ... pulsing and flowing ... Feel it now.

If you wish, imagine that the earth's heartbeat and yours are one ... beating in unison ... they seem to be one ... Feel that ... nourishing and strengthening your being ... regular, steady, calming ... know that herein is your life, the rhythm of life ... your connection, your rootedness with creation.

Remember that whenever you become aware of your heartbeat, you can always come back to this place, this sense of groundedness ... to this sense of rootedness ... calmness ...

centeredness . . . permit yourself to feel this connection to the planet, to the life-force.

Take an audible breath

Now imagine that there's a soft breeze blowing over you . . . There's just a hint of the cool sweetness of an early evening . . . Breathe in that freshness . . . that refreshment after a long day . . . Feel the soothing, cleansing, calming touch on your brow . . . Feel it smoothing out every trace of tension on your brow . . . around your eyes . . . mouth . . . jaw . . . and even around your ears . . . your scalp . . . released, smoothed.

Continue to breathe in that sweet freshness . . . calming . . . cleansing . . . refreshing . . . and remembering that you can, at any time, return to this totally relaxed, centered state.

Now imagine what it would be like if part of you could follow the breeze up into the air . . . lightly and gently . . . slowly and freely . . . over the grasses and the flowers and the sand . . . around the trees, following up, twirling up and gently around, ever so lightly.

And now allow yourself to follow the gentle breeze . . . and just become a part of it and rise up . . . floating up . . . higher and higher . . . until you are viewing the earth from above.

It feels so natural and comfortable . . . knowing that you're still being supported.

Now you can view the earth with a new perspective . . . What you've seen in pictures is now before you . . . a beautiful planet.

You can see the oceans . . . and forests . . . deserts . . . and mountains . . . and clouds . . . As you look, the details begin to blur into colors . . . georgeous blues . . . vibrant greens . . . deep browns . . . reds . . . and pure white . . . The colors change and blend as the sun shines at different angles . . . Notice the lights and shadows, the glorious interplay of light and colors . . . just look and enjoy what you are seeing.

Notice what you are feeling . . . Feel your response to what you are experiencing . . . Notice the feeling in your heart.

Imagine that you can see a thread of light flowing from your heart toward the earth . . . connecting you to the earth . . . It connects you to the earth . . . to all your fellow creatures on the earth . . . and the light flows back to you along this thread . . . flowing, filling you with brightness . . . reassurance . . . connection.

Your whole being responds to its warmth and you seem to glow.

And as the brightness grows in you, notice that the light glows brighter around the earth . . . It expands around the earth . . . It seems to expand outward . . . gently . . . until you are enveloped in it . . . It bathes you, caresses you . . . You slowly begin to realize that the light within you is the same as the light around you . . . the light from your heart is the same as the light around you . . . It's all the same.

You notice that this light around you continues to expand and extend outward into space, possibly into the whole universe . . . Everything is encompassed in this light . . . you feel the connectedness . . . You are a part of it . . . You are linked with everything . . . in this light . . . through this light . . . through the light in your being . . . the light in your heart . . . See it . . . Notice it . . . Feel it.

Now as you float and experience this joy . . . comfort . . . oneness . . . You may slowly begin to come back whenever you are ready . . . Whenever you wish, slowly come back . . . ever so gently . . . down to the earth . . . until you are right back in your body on the earth . . . Feeling your body pressing against the earth . . . against the floor . . . comfortable and at home . . . secure and connected.

And as you take a breath, you know that as you wake up, you can carry this experience, this vision, with you . . . and know that it is a part of everyone . . . You feel happy and content and very much at home.

Pause

Slowly bring your awareness back to this room, to this place of yours on the earth . . . and when you are ready, gently open your eyes . . . knowing that this place on the earth is always here for you . . . is always with you . . . nourishing and comforting you.

Repeat the above instruction until everyone is alert.

Contributors

Judd Allen, Ph.D. Human Resources Institute, 115 Dunder Rd., Burlington, VT 05401. 802/862-8855. E-mail: JuddA@healthyculture.com. Web site: www.healthyculture.com. Psychologist, author, and consultant, Judd specializes in helping businesses and communities build supportive cultural environments. Judd serves as president of Human Resources Institute and as an editor of *The American Journal of Health Promotion.*

Donald B. Ardell, Ph.D. 345 Bayshore Blvd., #414, Tampa, FL 33606. 813/241-4567. E-mail: Donardell@earthlink.net. Don wrote the landmark book *High Level Wellness: An Alternative to Doctors, Drugs, and Disease,* as well as several well-known books on wellness. He now serves as host for a weekly online wellness show (222.yourhealth.com). He also publishes the *Ardell Wellness Report.* Call or write Don for a free copy.

Michael Arloski, Ph.D. Arloski & Associates, 245 Redstone Dr., Bellvue, CO 80512. 970/484-3477. E-mail: arloski@frii.com. Michael is a licensed psychologist at the University Counseling Center, University of Northern Colorado. He directs Arloski & Associates offering speaking, training, and seminars nationally and internationally. Michael's unique blend of Eastern and Western holistic stress management methods has been enthusiastically received in the United States, Thailand, and at the National Wellness Conference. He is author of the *Stress Thrivers Relax Pack,* a two cassette relaxation/stress management training package. Michael is a past president of the Colorado College Counselors Association and the Ohio Society for Behavioral Health and Biofeedback.

James E. Borling, M.M., MT-BC, SAMI. Department of Music, Radford University, Radford, VA 24142. 504/831-5177. Jim is the director of the Music Therapy Program at Radford University in Radford, Virginia. He received the title of fellow from the Association for Music and Imagery and makes use of Music Evoked Imagery in his private practice in Roanoke, Virginia.

Richard Boyum, Ed.D., Senior Psychologist and Associate Professor, University of Wisconsin-Eau Claire, Center for Academic, Personal and Career Development, Eau Claire, WI, 54702-4004. 715/836-5050.

Bob Czimbal. Healthworks, 2501 SE Madison, Portland, OR 97214. 503/232-3522. As director of HEALTHWORKS, Bob implements workplace wellness programs and develops products. As a national keynote speaker and trainer, Bob's presentation titles include Enhancing Self-Esteem, Friends and Fun, Laughing at Life, Motivation at Work, Yes to Life . . . Wellness! and Vitamin T.

Bob Fellows, M.T.S. Mind Matters, Inc. P.O. Box 16557, Minneapolis, MN 55416. 612/925-4090. Bob is a professional mentalist, illusionist, and educational consultant with a Master of Theological Studies from Harvard University. Fellows regularly gives presentations dealing with wellness and self-responsibility to students, educators, employees, executives, and national television audiences in the United States, Canada, and Australia. He is the author of *Easily Fooled: New Insights and Techniques for Resisting Manipulation.*

Tom Ferguson, M.D. Self-Care Productions, 3805 Stevenson Ave., Austin, TX 78703. 512/472-1333. E-mail: DrTomHi@aol.com. Tom is a self-care pioneer. He is president of Self-Care Productions in Austin, Texas, and is a senior associate at Harvard Medical School's Center for Clinical Computing. He founded the influential journal *Medical Self-Care* and is medical editor of the *Whole Earth Catalog*. In his book *Megatrends*, author John Naisbitt cited his work as representing "the essence of the shift from institutional help to self-help." Tom has recently been involved in organizing the United State's first series of conferences on consumer health informatics—the study and development of computer systems that support the informed, proactive health consumer. His newest book is *Health Online: How to Find Health Information, Support Forums, and Self-Help Communities in Cyberspace* (Addison-Wesley, 1996).

Judy A. Fulop, M.S., N.D. (1999) Natural Paths to Health, 2140 Laurel Woods, Salem, VA 24153. 503/231-7786. Judy is currently pursuing her dream of becoming a naturopathic physician at the National College of Naturopathic Medicine in Portland, Oregon. She speaks and consults nationally and internationally on guided imagery, psychoneuroimmunology, women's health, and natural medicine. She was formerly the director of Well Life at Saint Joseph Health Center in Kansas City, Missouri, where she integrated wellness within the medical setting so that the community, patients, staff, and physicians could benefit from wellness in the healing process.

Bob Haywood III. University of North Carolina at Wilmington, 601 South College Rd., Wilmington, NC 28403. 919/799-8497. Bob, a campus minister for twenty-six years, has led numerous workshops and groups in Spiritual Wellness. He enjoys leading personal growth and wellness cruises to the Bahamas.

Deborah Haywood, M.S., CHES. University of North Carolina at Wilmington, 601 South College Rd., Wilmington, NC 28403. 910/962-4137. Deborah has worked as the director for the UNCW Wellness Promotion Center for the last twelve years, teaches a course in Individual Well-Being, and coleads personal growth and wellness cruises for students.

John Heil, D.A. Lewis-Gale Clinic, 4910 Valley View Blvd., Roanoke, VA 24012. 540/265-1605. John is a psychologist specializing in sport psychology and behavioral medicine. He is coordinator of Psychological Services for Lewis-Gale Hospital Pain Management Center and provides sport psychology consultation to the Commonwealth Games of Virginia, the U.S. Fencing Association, the Committee on Sports Equipment and Facilities, and the Virginia Amateur Sports Association.

Constance C. Kirk, Ed.D. 381 West Ann, Whitewater, WI 53190. 414/473-5761. Connie is an assistant professor in health education at the University of Wisconsin-Whitewater. She has designed programs to facilitate behavior change and conducts seminars in weight dynamics, using language for high level performance and imagery for healing. She is the author of *Taming the Diet Dragon: Using Language and Imagery for Weight Control and Body Transformation.*

Barbara Kyle, M.Ed. P.O. Box 973, Salem, VA 24153. 703/389-1870. Barbara is a retired educator and high school guidance counselor. She is now an active certified yoga instructor.

Karen G. Lane, M.Ed. 2628 Sweetbrier Ave. SW, Roanoke, VA 24015. 540/989-1304. Karen is actively involved in community education as a master gardener and uses gardening as meditation and therapy. Karen has led and participated in various meditation and prayer groups. She conducts research for the Medical College of Virginia and is a student of Process Oriented Psychology.

Julie T. Lusk, M.Ed., L.P.C., C.Y.I. c/o Whole Person Associates, 210 West Michigan, Duluth, MN 55802-1908. 218/727-0500. E-mail: JTLusk@aol.com. Julie is the director of the Health Management Center at Lewis-Gale Clinic in Salem, Virginia. She develops wellness programs for businesses, colleges, and communities and is widely known nationally and internationally for her workshops on a variety of mind/body topics. She has taught yoga since 1977 and is the creator of *Desktop Yoga* (Putnam Perigee Books).

Lauve Metcalfe, M.S. 450 W. Valle Del Oro, Tuscon, AZ 85737. 520/742-1012. Lauve is an internationally known health and lifestyle consultant specializing in seminars, workshops, and corporate health program development. She has led wellness programs at Canyon Ranch Resort, Campbell Soup, the United States Army, and the state of Florida. She is a triathlete and marathon runner.

Patricia A. McPartland, MS, MCRP, Ed.D. C.Ht., C.Ha. Southeastern Massachusetts Area Health Education Center (SMAHEC) Inc., P.O. Box 280, Marion, MA 02738. 508/748-0837. Patricia is an internationally known educator, writer, and lecturer and the executive director of SMAHEC, an organization that focuses on cross cultural competency training. She is certified in holistic aromatherapy and hypnotherapy and is the author of *Promoting Health in the Workplace*. Patricia also conducts workshops on marketing, stress management, healing, aromatherapy, and maximizing your potential and is available for private consultation.

Don Powell, Ph.D. 30445 Northwestern Hwy., Suite 350, Farmington Hills, MI 48334. 810/539-7800. Don is president of the American Institute for Preventive Medicine and an international leader of wellness programs with over 1500 clients using its materials. He is considered to be one of the country's foremost authorities on the design, marketing, and implementation of community and corporate health education programs. Don is the author of *365 Health Hints and Self-Care: Your Family Guide to Symptoms and How to Treat Them*.

Walt Schafer, Ph.D. 5357 Nimshew Run, Chico, CA 95928. Walt is the author of *Stress Management for Wellness, Second Edition*, Fort Worth: Harcourt, Brace and Jovanovich.

Judy Schwakopf, B.A. in Nursing. St. Joseph Health Center, 1000 Carondelet Dr., Kansas City, MO 64114. Judy is a Childbirth Education Coordinator and Educator. She is a member of the Association of Women's Health, Obstetric, and Neonatal Nurses, and Kansas City Area Childbirth Educators and is a mother of four.

Bernie Siegel, M.D. ECaP. 300 Plaza Middlesex, Middletown, CT 06457. Bernie is a pediatric and general surgeon. In 1978 he started Exceptional Cancer patients, a specific form of individual and group therapy utilizing patients' dreams, drawings, and images. Bernie is involved in humanizing medical education and making the medical profession and patients aware of the mind-body connection. He is the author of *Love, Medicine and Miracles* and *Peace, Love and Healing* and *How to Live Between Office Visits*. His guided meditations are available on audiotape through Hay House, 1154 Dominguez St., P.O. Box 6204, Carson, CA 90749. 800/654-1526.

Karen Sothers, M.Ed. 12275-126 Carmel Vista Rd., San Diego, CA 92130. 619/481-2251. Karen is a health and lifestyle consultant with ScrippsHealth and the LaCosta Resort and Spa in San Diego. She is also the Stress Management Specialist for the Dr. Dean Ornish Reversing Heart Disease Program at ScrippsHealth. As a certified yoga instructor, Karen teaches yoga, meditation, and relaxation training, as well as stress reduction and weight control.

Debbie Stevens. 607 Walnut Ave. SE, Roanoke, VA 24014. 540/427-4632. Debbie has a background in social work and has been teaching yoga since 1988. Debbie is a certified yoga instructor and is a Phoenix Rising Yoga Therapy practitioner. In 1998, she opened The Yoga

Center in Roanoke, Virginia. Debbie has made guided imagery, yoga, and relaxation audiotapes.

Tom Tapin. c/o 2140 Laurel Woods, Salem, VA 24153. Tom lives in South America where he is implementing new technologies that dramatically reduces waste generated in drilling oil and gas wells. He has lived all around the world and consults internationally. Tom states that the recent big events of his life are a direct result of creative visualization and a few blessings. He is a source of inspiration to all who meet him, and especially to Julie Lusk, his sister. He believes that if you are going to dream, dream big.

Donald A. Tubesing, M.Div., Ph.D. Whole Person Associates, 210 W Michigan St., Duluth, MN 55802-1908. 218/727-0500. Web site: www.wholeperson.com. Don is a pioneer in the fields of stress management and wellness promotion. *Seeking Your Healthy Balance* and *Kicking Your Stress Habits* are his most popular books. Don's company, Whole Person Associates, publishes a wide variety of materials for trainers. Write or call for a free catalog.

John Zach, M.S. University of Wisconsin-Stevens Point, Career Services, 134 Old Main, Stevens Point, WI 54481. 715/346-3226. John is a career counselor/therapist in the Career Services Offices at the University of Wisconsin-Stevens Point. Since 1975, John has provided training in the use of imagery in the areas of wellness, career development, and personal improvement.

Maggie Zadikov. Healthworks, 2501 SE Madison, Portland, OR 97214. 503/232-3522. Maggie began a 12 year career as an elementary school teacher where she integrated Vitamin T (Healthy Touch) and guided imagery into her work with children. She is an experienced presenter of relaxation skills, massage, eating, weight issues, and Vitamin T. Maggie is currently an acupuncturist practicing in Portland, Oregon.

Cross-Reference Index

The scripts from volumes 1 and 2 have been organized into the following categories to help you select the ones that are most appropriate for the issues you and your clients are working on. You'll find that certain scripts are listed under more than one category.